10⁻

5

Year of the Propaganda-Corrupted Eclipse

NEW RIVER PRESS YEARBOOK 2017/2018

Copyright © NEW RIVER PRESS
This first edition published in 2017
by New River Press London

thenewriverpress.com

Edited by Heathcote Ruthven
set in Mrs Eaves
design and typesetting
by New River Press

Cover image:
Robert Montgomery, *Estuary Poem for Wyndham Lewis. 2017*

New River Press is an indie poetry press based in Fitzrovia,
London. It publishes new work by new and established poets,
and the *New River Press Yearbook* annually.

ISBN: 978-0-9954807-9-7

P
O
E
T
S

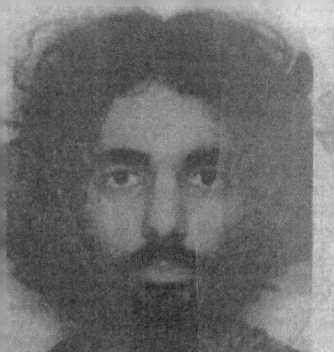

Zia Amead

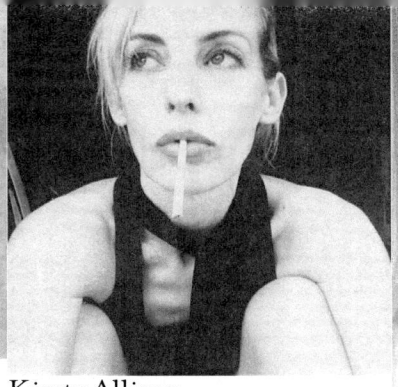

Kirsty Allison

Louise Androlia

Zack Ashley

Earl James Atkinson

Rhiannon Auriol

Ione Azura

Joe Ball

Victoria Bartley

Benny Bellamacina

Greta Bellamacina

Greta Bellamacina &
Robert Montgomery

Jaclyn Bethany

Merlin Betts

Katie Byrne

Natalie Carr

Lily Cheifetz-Fong

Sorcha Collister

Phoebe Corbett

Christian Corcoran

Pele Cox

Miguel Cullen

Kirilia Cvetkovska

Stephanie Czapla

Miranda Darling

Lillie Davidson

Pauline de Drouas

Charles Derenne

Jeramy Dodds

Britanny Drays

Oscar Dunbar

David Erdos

Suzy Feay

Sophie Fenella

John Finnigan

Jane Angeles Fitton

Maria Gazis

Frankie Glace

Salena Godden

Oliver Gomm

Sinead Graham

Lily Guy-Vogel

Svetlana Grishina

Regina Gunapranata

Charlotte Hanger

Alastair Hodgen

Michael Horovitz
photo David Trainer

Vanessa Vie &
Michael Horovtiz

Julia Houghton

Rosalind Jana

Miranda Keyes

Louise King

Lara Konrad

Elena Larrson

Mathilde Leblond

Jamie Lee

Robert Lundquist

Lisa Luxx

Damian Madden

Eleanor Malbon

Anika Valentina Maric

James Massiah

Chris McCabe

Devin Taylor McCarthy

Niall McDevitt

Tabitha McKinney

Tenishia McSweeney

Amy Lou Miller

Lilli Moors

Robert Montgomery

Nick Moss

Sophie Naufal-Baker

Elizabeth O'Connor

Hande Oynar

Kayleigh Parle

Verity Pemberton

Eleanor Perry-Smith

Margaret Perry

Barbara Polla

Mick Ray

Edd Ravn

Jeremy Reed

Anna Rieser

Rebecca Mary Rose

Onur Safak

Sebastian Sanchez-Schilling

Stefanie Schefter

Oliver Schick

Jennifer Francesca
Sciuchetti

Ana Seferovic

Afshan Shafi

Ásta Sigurðardóttir

Amber Singh

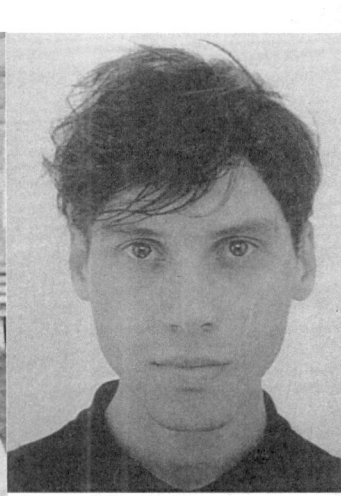

Pollie Sortain

Scott Temple

Ramo Thek-Zerouai

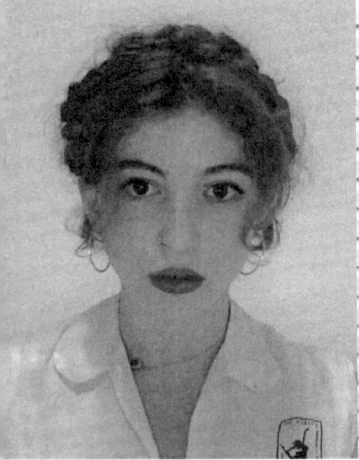

Sophie Thompson

Poppy Turner

Cecilia Valensise

Vanessa Vie

Saira Viola

David Walker

Mariana Saori Wall

Lori Wallace

Emily Wells

Cecily Whitehead

Alice Whiting

Elizabeth Jane Whitton

Simon Widdop

Heathcote Williams

Jan Woolf

Hugo Zeehyena

YEAR OF THE PROPAGANDA-CORRUPTED PLEBISCITES

Reading all these poems will give you the most painful and wonderful longing to meet the people who wrote them. As they came flooding into the New River inbox we had the illicit feeling of reading the cut up pages from a thousand intense strangers' diaries. And a thousand intense friends' diaries. Intimacy and the unknown and the strident and the witty commingle in this collaborative portrait of 2017.

The poets are in rough alphabetical order, which, like when you're lined up by name at the school fire drill, produced some lovely pairings: Old friends Jan Woolf (playwright, novelist, activist) and Heathcote Williams lurk in the back, etching anti-war graffiti onto the bins; academic overachievers Pele Cox (poet in residence at both the Tate and RA) and Miguel Cullen (founder of Odilo Press) surprise each other with stories of their secret wild sides; rock star Jamie Lee receives some much need-ed therapy from practicing psychoanalyst Robert Lundquist; New River's own '70s chic genius superpoet Rosalind Jana and the mysterious artist Miranda Keyes plan icy swimming expedi-tions; while Greta Bellamacina and her father Benny Bellamac-ina joyously yelp renditions of Kinks songs while tap dancing. Greta's enchants all with her rallying cry 'Tomorrow's Women'.

And all through the queue is frantic chatter about the great tragedies. Lisa Luxx and Niall McDevitt each provide powerful commentaries on Grenfell Tower, the estate in West London obliterated by a predictable – and predicted – inferno, caused by decades of criminal neglect by the local Tory council. Generations will tell and retell the story of Grenfell, and maybe out of its ashes a more decent society will emerge.

It gives cause to remember the independent state of squatters formed down the road from Grenfell in the 1970s, Frestonia. With the late Heathcote Williams acting as their ambassador to the United Kingdom, the collective applied to the UN for peacekeeping troops to protect them from the Greater London Council. In the surrounding streets phrases like "HOUSING IS A RIGHT - FREEDOM IS A CAREER", "WORDS DO NOT MEAN ANYTHING TODAY", and William Blake's "THE TIGERS OF WRATH ARE WISER THAN THE HORSES OF INSTRUCTION" were painted in bold colourful letters. Rebellious stunts and community spirit had their desired effect, and the majority squatters were offered social housing. Squatting was a powerful tool in the fight for tenants' rights. Their happy legacy is today under threat; we should study it carefully. Heathcote Williams died in July. His life is celebrated here with poems by Saira Viola, David Erdos, and Vanessa Vie. His book The Last Dodo and Dreams of Flying was published by New River Press in 2017.

We are extremely proud to have poems by old and new idols. Michael Horowitz, Jeremy Reed, and Jeramy Dodds are all heavyweights. There are at least two 20-year olds in the collection, Brittany Drays and Christian Corcoran, though you wouldn't know that from their poems. Drays writes serious and honest work with a raw economy. Corcoran is accomplished and wild. The wonder that is Afshan Shafi contributes two highlights about magical animals. Zia Ahmed has all the wit of a modern day Larkin. Read his piece out loud. Read them all aloud. Ana Seferovic is a Belgrade-born surrealist 'genre fluid' text artist whose poem The Magnificent Sunset Of Thrills has no original language - the English is translated from the Serbian, and the Serbian from the English. She embodies the breaking apart of borders into the transcendental.

The collaborative poem Seven Sisters by Greta Bellamacina and Robert Montgomery is a snapshot of the year of Brexit and Trump in 7 characters. The mania of images in Jeremy Dodds work has all the energetic discord of a Modernist symphony. Barbara Polla's visceral love filth is like nothing you've ever read.

Perhaps the gem of the whole collection is Too Serious by Lily Cheifetz-Fong, a preternaturally talented 11-year old from London, who might just be the new Mozart of war poetry. We should all learn her words by heart until our hearts explode.

Hope runs through this book like an underground river. Our enemies may be in power, but hope is not dead. Only kindness will save us now. The Trump government and the Brexiteers are not our future, they are just the panicked last gasp of failed ideologies. From the new generation a Psychic Love Wave will explode across all countries. In our new world refugees will be given shelter, immigrants will be hugged in the streets we will run kissing through the streets next summer and paradise will take over the city. We can already see the sunlight breaking through the trees above your rainbow smile.

New River Press.
London. December 2017

CONTENTS

Home- Zia Ahmed

i'm running running like thoughts running from
thoughts rattling from the constant battling broken pieces
floating tokens token gestures token jester open sesame
ali baba forty thieves forty grievances nothing to pledge
allegiance with trapped in a box ballerina chopped off
for bhangra man dance monkey dance to the music of the
snake charmer i am karma i am kama sutra i am ni tu hune
hune hoi mutiyar mundian to bach ke rahin i am your gap
year you said you were lost i hope you found yourself i am
slumdog millionaire downward dog eight headed god i am
shiva al-qaeda i am auditioning for the role of terrorist
one yes i can do that in an arabic accent i am dhalsim i am
bollywood season on channel four at two in the morning
i am ganges i am gandhi i am jinnah i am five pillars i am
sinner i am cinnamon i am cardamom i am not invited to
the houses of parliament i am sharif don't like it rock the
casbah stop the fatwa allahu akbar allahu akbar la illa ha
illalah i am england no you're not mate look at your face i
am england shirt made in bangladesh i am brick lane i am
curry house of the year two thousand and five i am rogan
josh i am so damn lost i am so damn lost just looking for a
place that's home
looking for a shape that's whole mera joota hai japani
home is where your heart is yeh patloon inglastani nah
home is where your heart lifts sar pe lal topi russi nah
home is where your arse fits phir bhi dil hai nah home is
where you're ok to stay till you leave in a casket
phir bhi dil hai...

Cultural Traffic – Kirsty Allison

I'm giving you an hour
The hour wasted on social
yesterday stuck
on this train
From Shelter to Desperation
To Wonder Lattes
Share the seat
I do not
No prisoners
No passengers
Pass glass balconies,
 flats by the Thames –
 million pound boxes –
spectrum of washing up bubble flare in the morning light
Disney castle dreams
shunt enslaved
On unicorns
To pray at Laksmi's fountain
I'm dressed for war
Just wanna have a look, do you?
Share luminous wallet
Black out
I wanna back out
Operating system malfunction
Deplete. Power.
We are everything
We are everywhere
I am everything
I am everywhere
We are our gods
I am my god
Are you my god?
God is me
Is you
You are me

Am I you?
You are not my shaman
You are not my people
I am not your content
Do not dilute
What i still have of me.

Inside World - Kirsty Allison

Going out like an outpatient
Horseless cowboys own the room
So drunk they can hardly talk.
Backdoor it
Go.
Eagle gimp Mask
autumnal head –
Magpie batteries to your nest
Compost gold scattered leaves
ET should not be fucking a dog
There is no tea trolley in the taxi
Add candles incense roses
Stay in – slab mortuary style

Skin - Kirsty Allison

We killed birds
Needless roll of the death scroll
We are children of data
Binary babies
Monsters marching under the burning sun
We are poachers
Poachers
Without laughter lines
We fill the wifi sky
We are screen grabbed simulacrum
We are the anthropocene generation
Ascetics: hung, drawn, slaughtered
Kill or be killed
We are no pixel victims
Yet teeth chip
Under the cashmere filter
We are the starling crowd
Vagrants mugging winged data
We must kill the birds
Or we will be pecked alive

Untitled - Louise Androlia

I.

Your body
Is
Mostly water
-
You have
Tears
To spare.

2.

Under all these layers
I settle down
Amongst
Blankets
Of myself.

3.

Good morning to these
New memories
That are already
Fading from view.

4.

Fractured time stands still
I wonder where I have gone
But the world still spins.

I'm Selfish - Zack Ashley

My air is being touched
touched by youth
touched by a dark knight
touched by the rich in happiness
drinking me dry.
My air is for the writer
the wild from time to time
not those who preach
or binge on Beethoven;
but after I roll away
I listen and learn
from their smart but sly
one-man mission:
"that we are the same"
when we are not the same.
Again and again
man to man we float,
disguised in a skinless suit —
that time,
a timed rant about the mix of races,
this turmoil Iraq
just dropped
like
an orange in a hat...
dare to criticize?
as one sits,
messed up like a flower
with pneumonia —
or an instrumental rape.

Bad Friend – Earl James Atkinson

I only left so i could come back and get you
it's been 10 years
and I hate that I left you

regret and loss
in exchange for successful

moving alone
is growing more stressful

but this the choice I made
it's the kind voices, I forsake
I take
took for granted

replaced, disgraced, supplanted

with upgrades, parades and parties

now I'm hungry, ashamed and frightened
always looking and striving
for a life less violent
for love and the next horizon

All Apologies. Bad Friend ii. Pret Grovsner Square – Earl James Atkinson

I'm sorry I missed your birthday
I still love you
I wasn't able
I needed
had to
rest and regroup
I count deal with a group

I'm sorry I couldn't come to the show
I can't afford oysters
my minds feeling uber slow
hard times for me
I can't afford to be
involved right now
soon and how

I'm sorry I wasn't at the marathon
please carry on
I cary the guilt around
I wear it on my face
in my voice
you can hear the choices I made
I can't be in all places
at all times
but
I'll be there
at the finish line....

Touch - Rhiannon Bartley

i.
I'm new to this.
birmingham in the morning.
a perfect moon
clatters against the face of evening.

ii.
 the fire brigade is out.
& will you sit with us in the fire of sunset

because who knew if life could be this pretty?

blood moon caught in scaffold ring
your eyes
the milk has run out
you wipe my chin
I do wish you were gentle

iv.
now, every evening when the bus passes I pray they may be
on it

and my understanding is like this:
of dimly lit bodies in the breath of sharp
you know me barely

                    capable
                dishonest
                    ravish this
v.

            a synaptic wave;
            my how we have grown,
            seeded ourselves into separate cities,
            blown far blown wide
            on the wind across oceans, kiss me!

Aqua Vitae - Rhiannon Auriol

him at fourteen grey eyed
schoolyard by the bins
backed up emptied

fifteen, a busy year
she was beautiful but
so sad

we all lost a lot
from our experiences
of sixteenth living
at number 49 that time

honed my unique
skill-set
as an intern, he
could have been my age
in the dark

moving on, started
earning from it
for a while it was pure

left school and now oh
things got rougher

names, names, names
you, my love

Three Untitled Poems — Ione Azura

i

Mind is the egg splits
Push fingers in grey yellow slit
Man is pink brown putty
Gutter us
Empty
An ease I call
I wash lilies
Bring to pass
Place my head my hands at his feet
Pushing my cheeks over his calves.

ii

We made a meal from us
We made a meal and ate it too quickly
We suffered indigestion burping and holding out belly
It was us
We licked us clean and now we have nothing left
We should have eaten more slowly.

iii

My shoelace swings around my ankle as i walk
It is the shoelace of the merciless
Catching in my chain as I try to keep time
A rattle speaks to me
I take up serpents on sandy shores
I drink a deadly thing until I die
God moves up on me
Servant devil visionary
A soft squirt
Another kind of bible
He strikes a man
He strikes a woman
And shum shum shtick tongue
It is from here I am carried on my final journey. To the
hammam meat cafe
Red light apocolypse vacation interest
It is yellow dusk and I have become an iron corpse, col-
ourless and deranged
There is a man
He is inspector outlet
He plays the disorder game
Eye wild zero gravity
He is walking in circles screaming to Mohammed
Yolk hits his bare toes
I fall on my hands and knees
This is an act of passing
Pass for, pass off, pass out.

Ode To Harland - Joe Ball

How time moves on eh
I'm still dealing with junkies from a council estate
And you've got your arms around someone in Tatler
I thinking we're dealing in different circles.
Still spinning, still spinning, still spinning
You and your book covers
And me in the midst
All poetic landscapes forgot
Funny quips though
Yeh it's like that up here
Still a gang of fuckin jokers
Snakeskin shoes and no fuckin socks
Pop the champagne corks
It's sunny at the coast
I might see you around
Out on the pavement
Share a cig
Or maybe not

The Day Before Armistice Day - Joe Ball

Tomorrow their will be berets and salutes
Wheelchairs and dignitaries
Wreaths of paper poppies

He whispers the names recorded in stone
Tommy, Laurie, Howard, Jack
Shallows in stone

He remembers stealing a kiss from Tommy's girlfriend
Behind the Durning Arms after closing
He can taste it now, sweet with longing and still not bitter
yet regret
She asked him what she was to do now Tommy was gone
He walked her home and kissed her by the gate
Before her mother caught up.

May sits in the armchair
beautiful as her name alludes
As time takes her memory
"Do we go out tonight Albert"
"Not tonight love, it's Saturday"
"I thought we went out tonight, dancing.
I'll get you moving."
The television is blaring at volume 40

He opens the French windows and steps into the fields of
memory
He hears the crack of shells above his head,
the rutting of earth, the splintering of bone.
All this noise, all this din.
A dog barks and he starts.
The garden beds need clearing,
he had told her not to plant the wild poppies
They take over, there are masses of them
He pulls at them
scattering petals across the ground

Shrewsbury II - Victoria Bartley

They say a man's home is his castle
But I have two homes now
The one my mother lives in
And the one your mother lives in

So our castle is built on the thick cloths
and polished wood
of restaurant tables
And wet streets
On the cocktail napkins
And the ride to work

Passenger seat silences cut short
by the radio
Comfortable
And uncomfortable

Our castle is built on the pages of
lonely planet books
In the windows of estate agents
And job searches on the internet

Shredded beer mats and old wine bottles
Scattered wax fingerprints
And your face dancing
behind the makeshift candle

Carving out brief privacy
In pub corners
And empty supermarket aisles

They say a man's home is his castle
But I have two homes now
The one my mother lives in
And the one your mother lives in

My Publisher – Benny Bellamacina

I read my new poem
to a publisher friend of mine
he replied
"It's a load of old tripe"
I thought you swine.

The very next day
I ready him two more
he quickly showed me
his publisher's door.

I then posted him a poem
I thought a load of tripe
"I love it"
he announced
then used it to light his publisher's pipe.

That Fool - Benny Bellamacina

The biggest fool
I ever knew
sat down next to me
on a pew

as I moved my head
he did too
and when I looked at his foot
he was wearing my shoe

so I turned away
and to my surprise
when I turned back
he looked me straight in the eyes

I thought how strange
what should I do?
Then the mirror said
"you fool, that fool is you".

Tomorrow's Woman - Greta Bellamacina

Tomorrow's woman has seen war in heaven
she is the blue of light before rain draws
she has watched the women
she loves turn to crashing stones
and not know how to swim.
above the stars that cannot be filmed
stars that are not known as paradise
known for their isolation
biographers of pain
too full of memory.
Tomorrow's woman is the colour of night
tomorrow's woman is your child
tomorrow's woman is shelter
she is sex
the last shock against death
sex the last peace
sex that forgets black and white
she is the first to hold a bird in her hands
and learn of foreign love
and not melt at the idea of difference.
Tomorrow's woman is too fat
she bleeds because she knows what it is to feel
a whole generation on her hips
and still be seen as empty
a dog
an ocean of plastic
a war child.
Face on a stand
eyes too close together
mouth like a rental car
feet crossed
the oven is on.
Tomorrow's woman is your father
and his mother and his mother and his mother

she is undammable,
a renaissance of marching women
we stand together
as strong as morning
as fearless as water
a school in the wind lighting
hands like stolen trees
stuck up in the fog
A library card to Jerusalem
only human in waves
a courtyard of scarlet fire
closed so far down into itself
it's hard to imagine what kind of God could believe
the dead sea was female
it's hard to imagine what kind of God could believe
that you could float on your back like this
not drowning.

Afterlight - Greta Bellamacina

We found out that Leonard Cohen died this morning
and the world was reminded about poetry
the pale domes of white light
all singing faraway from where we sleep

flame-shadowing gods everywhere
down the Tottenham Court Road
trapped up in treelight
lost in the light of the kitchen

you hold onto me and say
where do they go, the torpedoing shadows that fill the
world
where the moon tries to draw closer and touch love,
but doesn't quite make it through the fog.

And how death could be the only way to reunite
and return to music, and find a different kind of peace,
again how the angels must have known already
without the intent of prayers

the long long afterlight
stored up in the day,
shattering the harshness of the blank world.
But still it rains at home.

Like you, poetry still haunts everyone
like the way we brought our baby home from the hospital
all blue and breathed up
covered in traffic, a swaying heaven ship

the new cold in the air of our flat
is gentle, a cradle of ships all resting
making the afterlight command
a nameless world, all static and in us

we all forgot to be homesick
unhurt by the thought of "paradise",
building empires in our heads, made-up of broken-up
light keys,
the way the word 'key' is aways rowing forward

pulling us towards the belief of unseen shores
moving us in, and making us mad again
walking near us, playing hell violins
But really moving us closer to our own need for love.

Love which is warred for
safer in the sky
closer to the birds
who know your dreams intimately.

I have woken up in a window
and existed from both sides.
the morning is a train
the afterlife is a horse

lovedreamed
Riding, riding, the sky to the sky
looking and pulled up
in the wilderness of the stars that are lit.

Arms wide open, so close
growing into the dark cupboard
a hyacinth stretching
out into the first daylight.

Afterwards (for Daisy Boyd) — Greta Bellamacina

Post-hearted and regretted
we find you already fallen

autumn always kills me
the trees let go silvering fierce

the show is on the ground
the sky is upturned

London is no longer famous
the children are buzzing fingertips

a paper bag of tears named Diana
ceremonial stone walls in your husbands name

cigarette end gasping a golden rope
an arrow of the past

I don't know how many times we've moved house
to find space for dreaming

all of our old letters remain the downpour
unable to disturb the living

Ophelia is in the wind somewhere on the coast
leaving the sand to announce its suffering

the summer before comes back to haunt us
abandoned crows

Bunhill Fields undated
the remains of lovers

prepared like a porcelain dinner
always promising and straggering.

Seven Sisters - Greta Bellamacina & Robert Montgomery

You are beside me, winter trees, a comrade to the world, a home, the TV is playing war, we hope for peaceful sunlight. A whole heart of blood, resting on a whole heart of blood.

The children are dressed in black, they are throwing petrol bombs at the embassies, throwing electric flowers into the graveyards of capitalism.

The philosopher is counting the slow candles of the icebergs, noting how many summers we have left. She is brilliant in her sunlight hat. Her chest is a pyramid.

The president has retreated to the golf club, he rules in half sentences. Coughing up the 1950s his mind is a puddle where broken dreams sit on the rooftops of libraries.

New weddings and empty churches, the minarets talk to the dawn before the sun lights up the city. The priests are whirling like dervishes in circles, they pinball off the walls, singing silence.

Diana and the swan ride an open topped red London bus, the trumpets beside them play rave music, LSD trips to the sound of brass bands. CCTV diamonds for Oyster cards.

God is bored of us now. She sides with the animals and the weather and they watch our digital alien rampage, with cool sad eyes.

Untitled - Jaclyn Bethany

midnight sun of weeping willows
a country an ocean away
no woods, just light
a valley with pink clouds that quickly turn to grey
full of desire
and lust
a river, a spring
winding
like the crossroads
that bind together
each new place
a prayer, a different world
fragments left across the burning mountain
waiting to be redeemed
something we long to understand

it is not the same
it will never be the same

Sunken Astroboy — Merlin Betts

You walk over ashen-faced waters languid
In sunlight, the featureless mass glassed a thousand times
Weekly: gently tumble onto the bow with that
Nearly-died-but-didn't giggle wheezing betwixt
Bright pink lips pursing and settle into an easy
Chair of rotted leather, swathed in fun fur — of course
It's good to see you — where

Wilful postulations around the subject of farts
Bring an ellerdine tranquility to the dereliction
Of home comforts: smells of motor oil, fish
And excrement, alternately bringing me
Conclusions of the wandering sentiment
That I'm your fast pedal Fuzzbox, your gilt hyena,
Your Quodrophenia, your Swedish Astrodoll in the long
cold night -
These niche incantations and silverthread joy:
Like a suckling bottleneck

I want to touch your hoodie — Merlin Betts

Down the canalside, mounting rubber dinghies
Among the paraphernalia of incontinence,
We have the shining glass shards from nearby
Office towers, cowering in booze from the babies
On the bank; demanding sugarpills and holy embrace
They sing a wordless melody of near-vomit hiccups
Extolling these, life's flamboyant virtues: it dribbles
Through the window down the bowls of my earholes
And flushes while the boat floats

There or here — Merlin Betts

Something quivers amid the elastane blend fabrics;
Your hands engage it like tongs considering a lump
Of metal that might, eventually be called sword,
But only after furnacing in a sheath of fire: you
Never liked my medieval metaphors; and the balloon
Goes up, the skyrocket inclines toward the moon
In banal American movie symbolism of misogynistic
Idealism, which idea lays me out on the bed early,

Bubbling canal passing by while you're left unsatisfied
I think I remember a phrase from somewhere dank
And pleasant: I will go to the Cellar Door, the most
Beautiful phrase in the English language, tongue
Those words with their pink stalactite detailing,
Mouth the whole phrase into you with a seething cultured
Joy that tickles a bit round the edges...So lapping up
The canal I sink into the Cellar Door more meaningful
Than skyscrapers, more loving than rockets.

No One - Katie Byrne

bare feet on white walls
could not but answer when you called

wide awake just to let you in
could your lost love have found me again?

hidden in the limbo light
of passing past lovers, day & night

broken kisses by lost lips searching for a comfort missed

fingertips draw the space between this unbearable feeling
of what could have been

tears rest on mornings' eye
you always knew how to make me cry

slowly breaking side by side
as you mourn a love that isn't mine

it's all a dream. nothing is real.
close enough to touch but not to feel

laid to rest the silence dead our ghosts are aching
with what can't be said

hope is gone
forever is done
my phantom love the end has come

like the tide coming in
I finally see
we are strangers again only you. only me.

,,,

shouldn't have answered when you called but to feel this
pain
is better
than feeling

nothing at all

Bulbs - Natalie Carr

Whispering past the month,
All spring lies
Wrapped up in tissue paper likeness
All delicate and thin
Concealing the new,
Nestled and nestling.
The opening and closing of chapters
With a stouthearted performance.

A heaviness to day and night
Swapped for the bright
A changing of the guards
The palace like efficiency,
Days open up in hours
As the violet buds of the crocus lawn -
Tender hands.

Waiting
Patiently as saints
For some animated fount of light.
As they have waited under the earth
In cocoon slumbers
So wise and so young
A telling sign.

Still, innocence is theirs
They cherish it
In infantile knowingness.
Yet to feel the rains
Yet to be drawn down by winds
They do not mind the state of it
For they know what is to come.
When their concealment is burnt
And the light let in
They will thrive.

Too Serious... - Lily Cheifetz-Fong

White, cold bone,
The colour of the day of the dead masks hanging on the
wall,
Hanging like a visage with nothing behind it,
Nothing to think or to love, like parts of our world,
The masks we buy with gold, shimmering like the only
hope left in a Syrian family's money box,
To me a mask is a small luxury.

Amaryllis red dripping like serene dew drops onto the
ravaged remains of a life,
Ebbing through the cracks like a trickle of water seeps
hatred,
A mother desperately trying to gather the remains of a
ruined life and put them back together piece by piece.

My fingers clicked on the lettered keys,
Clinking heavy like a ball and chain,
They said I was too serious to beat their high market,
They said that no-one's fingers would be blackened from
the print of my 'seriousness',
Only after they read what they want to read would they
go and gasp, and wash their dirty fingers from the lying
print,
I know they are too scared to face the grim reality; to face
the fact that they are being lied to over and over,
So they lock the room swimming with lies.

My eyes begin to burn,
I know the truth,
I have seen the truth.

I have met the guards who stand like zombies; dead eyes
unblinking, faces emotionless,

And yet the truth prickles all over me,
The truth that Problems are ravenous and feed off fear,
The truth that people like me are promoting the creation
of their food;

That people like me are spreading false fear,
Somewhere at the Earth's core there lies an invisible
blender mixing all the world's problems and spitting them
out to the wrong people.

My fingers clank on the gleaming, laptop keys,
The keys that have the power to poison the country,
I can hear the sound of a nervous boy shaking like a new
born deer; the nervous clicking of the gun in time with
the clicking of my keys.

My world is in a silken shell,
A shell where the outside cannot harm me,
Every time I read my lies out loud I can feel the enamel of
the shell splitting,
I see glimpses of another world,
My eyes sting and like a fist I have to clench them closed
once more,
Again I feel my shell healing but deep down I have found
the key to my soul secret,
I know I am trying to block reality and fall back into fan-
tasy.

I have known the invisible tale woman who stalks around
the room,
I have worked in coalition with her churning out lies and
tales,
Her spidery, gnarled fingers have plucked at the keys,
She has leapt inside me and comforted me,
She has persuaded me to not rebel against lies
and reassured me that it is not that bad what I am doing,
That print doesn't lie,

The spidery, gnarled fingers were once mine a long time ago,
Now it is time I stabbed her heartless heart of twisted tales and false print.

"MARMITE CRISIS" is more important than children dying every day as a result of procrastination and hatred?
The tale woman has distorted people's minds,
It's okay for police to be asking a Muslim to take her burkini or head scarf off but not a nun to take off her habit,
The tale people have spread propaganda from the North Pole to South America.

Like a print, tale men and women have been duplicated throughout the globe.
Almost every time a journalist is recruited to work for the press, a tale man or woman is born,
Therefore, I think there is something I ought to say: I AM A TALE WOMAN,
Never again are they going to say I'm too truthful to beat their high market,
Never again are they going to say I need to tell white lies because you know what,
I RESIGN!

Patti - Sorcha Collister

Your inspiration, your motivation,
not through saviour,
or nobility, through normality,
meeting madness,
artistic chaos, a perfect ideal.

Has aged –

Advanced, become disenchanted,
insincere, flat.
Musings, of someone who is losing,
has seen too much,
years change, cares little.

The naive art –

An unperfected idea, swept,
beneath paper and writings,
beneath broken glass and photographs.
Memories, thoughts, the heaviest rocks in your pocket,
no fresh air, no grease of your glasses, your hair,
affected deal. Life.

Little Deaths - Phoebe L. Corbett

I wake to the limbs
Of a silver birch,
Stretching
From the roots of our house.

Through the net, leaves
Loom, twisting with breeze, still
Bound by October's false hope
And fragile light
For a few more days.

As I blink, opening,
Rising from the ends of some
Dream that led me to briefly forget,
I am reminded that in all
I have searched, there will be
Death, changing autumn leaves —

Burnt amber and peach
Before ash,
Before winter burial
In cold soil.

Within weeks,
The mound of grave
Will be covered with little deaths,
Or we could say, tree deaths.

Of course, the leaves don't know —

There's always renewal.

Honeysuckle Love - Phoebe L. Corbett

On a Sunday morning, you pour yourself into
this tattered blanket like syrup, and I beg to taste
your sweetness. You smile a knowing smile,
crooked and wise to my loving, as seasoned, now,
as you could expect honeysuckle in Spring.

Remember, lover, that as you yawn, pale
flowers bloom from the roots of your teeth and
I wish to be planted. Let me hide in there,
let me lie down in the soft blubber of your cheek
and backstroke through your honeyed insides.

I know I am difficult to love.
I know I sob like a grieving mother more days than I
smile,
and I have no skin of armour. I know my eggshell is hard-
er
to hold, that my cracked edges are weapons you did not see
coming. I was not to be expected.

But there is not a heartbeat I wouldn't pound to come
home to you,
to hang my heavy chin by the door of your ribcage,
and empty myself into your blanket arms.
Please, let me sleep in your bellybutton,
while you lull me with your honeysuckle love.

In the Morning - Phoebe L. Corbett

I think to this morning,
And mourn.

Our fired breath, this
Choke of neck, a moan
To the window. I watch
The frosted hedge and fraying
Concrete, the pussycat ambling
Through next door's mud, through
White sheets hanging to dry. They'll
Stay damp forever, in this heat,
I muse, clutching the radiator

(Fevered hands behind me, stray
Hairs stuck to my nape.)

I mourn. It will happen
Again, the thick, tender movement
And rosy joy beneath
Powder sky in December.

It will happen: I will mourn
And moan, fainter this time -
Gently forgetting the last,
With her.

Reflections Of Saint Francis - Christian Corcoran

when I am with you
my words
sleep
soundly
in
 silence:
(!)

reflections of saint francis

who have i been following all of these years ?

f o l l o wing

        bird

        drib

        drop

        drib

        drop   (bird shit__

heart stop
please god
        these hymns
are not
enough *cough
cough*
            (bird shit__ ass
            (birds hit__ glass

                            the last

thing that they see -
their reflections
before they die

                                             i

                            point broken necks
                            back toward the sky -
and still,
still i wonder why:

                     oh, if you are really up there, lord,
then why are you so far from the birds?

in bed during the storm:
cloud

---

when i leave my body | r a i n a i r a i n a i r a i n a i r a i
n a i r a i n a i r
will i recognize my body | a i n a i r a i n a i r a i n a
i r a i n a i r a i n a i r a

                            | i n a i r a i n a i r a i n a i
r a i n a i r a i n a i r a i
s l e e p without | n a i r a i n a i r a i n a i r
a i n a i r a i n a i r a i n
    y | a i r a i n a i r a i n a i r a i
n a i r a i n a i r a i n a
    e | i r a i n a i r a i n a i r a i
n a i r a i n a i r a i n a i
    s | n a i r a i n a i r a i n a i r
a i n a i r a i n a i r a i n

                            | r a i n a i r a i n a i r a i n
a i r a i n a i r a i n a i r
b | a i n a i r a i n a i r a i n a

i r a i n a i r a i n a i r a
l i n k | i n a i r a i n a i r a i n a i
r a i n a i r a i n a i r a i
                                               | n a i r a i n a i r a i n a i r
a i n a i r a i n a i r a i n
to the other side | a i r a i n a i r a i n a i r a i
n a i r a i n a i r a i n a

—-

the mind dances between the rain drops   \   fills
darkness with darkness

prison:
i i i i i i i i i
love
you
                    ^

               or,
how to write a love song
without the letter i

The Rules– Pele Cox

Ask for separate bedrooms, do your own thing.
Do not fall in love with him.
Take books, including a guide book, so you can explore
on your own if things
    get rocky.
Have a task, make sure he doesn't think you think it's a
holiday.
Take shades through which he cannot see your eyes. Take
your own money.
Be as blank as possible. Take a notebook to write in furi-
ously.
Think along the lines you know: 'Bikini', ' The Horizon',
'Poetry'.
Let him decide.
Buy him a novel.
Take more poetry.
Some barrier – SPF 65 (not just for your skin).
Don't text furiously, it's rude. Remember you are creating
another world with
    just one room.
Don't have the answers, they are up to him. Anyway, for
now it's you – and
    that is a silent thing.
Make him happy.
Think about your self – esteem and if you have any, cancel
him.

The Ritz-Carlton, Laguna Niguel — Pele Cox

He goes away.
he comes back, he goes away.
He takes me to another hotel.
It's higher, clearer, more beautiful, it is as if
our affair has been moved to a costlier ocean.
at low, cool, marble atrium, the dollars of footsteps and
orange blossom hoisted in their garlands higher than us
even. Everyone is in white, waiting as our car rounds the
bend,
a swarm of help. The valets come like large white butter-
flies. I have been lifted to a hand — made heaven
so visible it hurts: Wow, wow!! I said,
getting out of our black car into the white release of an
asylum
(millionaire America style). So this is love?
I will not leave this complex for three days. Then we are at
Reception. is is the part we hate, with the names again and
the silver rail with our bags, which hang like nylon meat,
to the lift.
Along the brown marble walkway we run. Ancient Rome,
Disney, Tutankhamun.
"So, Mr and Mrs Brown, are you enjoying your stay?"
"We're not married", we say.
Walking beside this man, we know what is true. For a mo-
ment he is our sect, takes us away from sense to this per-
fect white room, leads us
to lie along the white down of a bed.
I say, "Are you afraid of where you are?"
"I think I hold back," he says,
"But coming here is the opposite of that."

I – Pele Cox

I'm walking round like Alice in a five star hotel I go to the
pool in perpetual waiting,
                    watch the world curve under my blue hat,
swallow a poem or two – then out to the terrace to spot
whales.
This is a trance state,
wandering from room to room like a pampered wife, then
back upstairs – it's a holiday
not a life. I
put the key card in, slide up and down for Green
but it won't let me in, the light flashes Red for Stop
and Red again, I have come to the wrong room, there's no
guide
and my blue hat whispers,
"Why are you wearing me inside?"

Dia Tribe— Miguel Cullen

In Dartmouth Park, lives Heather — her dad, Lloyd is a reggae journalist-author. Her father's mates would go to sound system dances on Alexandra Park, where you can just see the London Eye from the ugly pub in Ally Pally, and the sky is still friable and gritted from the pollution of Camden and adds a weave to the sheets of air rolling off Ferme Park Road onto the hill. Lloyd would follow religiously Sir Bigga the President's sound, from Tottenham.

On one gilded retro night they danced under-age, Finsbury Park raggamuffins, eyes brightly shining, light glinting off the houses that slanted off the hill; they were friends with George Power from nearby on Granville road and would drink cans of Lilt and Hubba Bubba, wearing Farah slacks and FU's jeans at that sound system party, between Sir Bigga the President; or Papa B — Tottenham; Mighty Intrepid Sound from Finsbury Park; and Progressive Sound from Turnpike Lane.

Heather met Louis at Acland Burghley school. Louis' father Jonathon is an artist, covering their garden nearby on the grooved roads between Junction road and the Heath with naked papier mâché sculptures. His brother is a session musician for a big Wembley-stadium-playing band. He plays his own art pop at the Jazz Café. Louis is in a big north London hip-hop group.

Louis gets reviewed in a UK rap magazine, by Ed, the son of a newspaper editor. Ed lives with his family in a house nearby on Highbury Fields, and as a teen would drink glassy-looking vodka, playing on the Fields swings at night, with weed from inside a neighbour's white puffa-jacket. He would play football next to Marble Arch, bouncing the football off the columns, near where the

Duke of Hamilton died by the sword under the horse-chestnut tree in 1712. His mum was a famous ballet dancer who appeared in front of Queen Beatrice when he was at prep school; at that age he would wear Moschino and Karl Kani before gate-crashing Holly Branson's birthday party.

So Louis reads the review, and goes out to London Fields on a summery Saturday afternoon, and gives a copy to Daniel, who lives off Stoke Newington Church street, and works as a builder. He lives with his parents, who have a lot of C L R James, T S Eliot, Noam Chomsky in book-shelves. Daniel got Rodigan to play at a house party of his, he knows Paul Gilroy, all the big bods. He sees his friends often who would sleep on the roof of William Patten school in Clissold Park on summer's nights, he chats la at business men in pubs off Stoke Newington Church street on Derby Day, curly hair and sharp nose in profile, shoulders and chest lifted up and head angled slightly down.

Billy calls Daniel. He wants him to deliver in Chelsea. Daniel swerves across London westward in his creosote, red-winged Oldsmobile, moving down Hoxton street, past the old workhouse, down by the steel foundry on Shoreditch High Street, put-putting through the high street traffic lights. Toby is in the car with him, remembering what happened the night before: "So Nigel was in the pub, and he was talking to Mark and Tendai. Nigel's shouting across..." Toby says grinning, "...Across the table to Tendai. He went: 'Your cousin! You know Vera! Vera! In a wheelchair! Your cousin! Winston!! Winston!!!'"

Daniel's entered the Euston road, going past Camden Town Hall, where the first Carnival took place in 1959, organised by Michael X, blacklister of politicians and friends with Christine Keeler's wicked Jamaican drug-dealer beaus, enemy of John Profumo. The land it stands

on is all the ancient property of the Duchy of Bedford
— near the road burrowing from the east; Russell Square
to Mornington Crescent; where you can see the Heath
shining like a green crest in the afternoon — land worn
long on the deed titles of the Duchy's fascistic 12th heir,
Hastings Russell.

Billy lives in a flat on Justice Walk, just off Old Church
street, where the magnolia blossoms look like ink-dart
shuttlecocks; the air is so quiet you can hear sex perfectly
standing across the road on a quiet night. He is with Ma-
rina Wheeler, the Countess of Devon, who has a house in
Umbria with rows of pruned pines like slices of chocolate
cake.

Then he gets a cab, through Victoria, up St James's, pick-
ing up Bryan Ferry at White's, across Piccadilly, up Shaft-
esbury Avenue, up through the crippled duct of Holborn,
across the river of Blackfriars road, through the Peabody
estate buildings around Whitecross street, up through the
frayed rope connecting the City to Old Bethnal Green
road, Ravenscroft road, through Wellington Row, past the
ugly blocks west of Haggerston Park, onto Queensbridge
road and into London Fields.

 There he meets Alex, who lives in the big Nash-type
house with ivy creeping on either side of the door. His
uncle married a friend of the Earl of Devon's and his dad
worked for Rolling Stone. He wears a dark APC sweat-top
and a plain-black, Nike jumper. He's got the same name
as Alex, who moved into a big house in Victoria Park Vil-
lage. Her wall is covered with fashion pictures. She works
as fashion accessories assistant for Marie Claire. She went
out with a guy from Australia who was older than her at
uni. She used to wear a baseball cap with her pony tail
coming out above the adjustable strap. She sees the way
the water collects on the criss-cross railings in the park,

how it blows from them in the wind; how the moon has a cracked areola like the veins in a glass lampshade, how the angels furl their wings on the atom heads in metal.

She sees the glowering craw of the man, J-son, whose humour sparkles like a peony, his glistering eyes are halls of mirrors, he's played happy hardcore at free parties in Holborn, DJed at Bagleys.

She sees the flabby, embarrassing teeth of his sweet friend J Cree, who works for no reward and much pain in the threatening energy of the Hackney road; in carcasses of parks; for mark: a dapper; called J Nature; growing out of abasement into the state rooms of the White House; prince of marking doors with the alphabet; Ben Eine's assassinating king of pink-squalled walls.

These are the kings of Classical mythology, they are the Christs of the glowing city, pink as roses, medium-kings, shouting roots reggae into cravings, zoo'd:

NW5 to N2-2 to North-5, E8-North-16 to South-W-3 to SW1, W1, West-C-2, EC2A, to East-9, to E3, was it Ezra Pound that quoth, he be more free than ye, but Jasey is more gleeing than hee.

An Ode to the Street- Kirila Cvetkovska

I praise you in the midst of a troubled epoch.
While praising conjures upon loving.
And loving settles upon thirst.
I praise you in the midst
of an agitated population.
Where you sit on a stool of devotion.
And I dream on a bed
of sentimental pollution.
I praise you in the midst
of a distressed circle.
When we go round,
spinning in a fitted constipation.
And we pound hard.
But we spin harder
than pounding hard.
As if the spinning beats the hurting.
As if I hurt you
with a visionary thinking.
Not as if you pain me
with a tainted stare.
Not as if you
eradicate my belief.
Not as if you
were all the waterfalls
that made me roar.

Silence is the Screams of the Dead - Stephanie Czapla

You light a cigarette
And apologize for not being fun.
Hours later,
You worship my legs,
And knees-bent forward,
I whispered, "I love you."
I wish I said it louder.

The divot in your collarbone
And the space between
The end of your ribcage and your hipbone
Fit my lips perfectly.
You're so beautiful when you face me
And your hair feels softer than ever.
Locked in your eyes,
I think "I love you."
I still wonder how much I really do.

You call yourself a lizard,
But I don't feel scales.
Nietzsche envies your nihilism,
But he doesn't know the heart you wield.
Face-down on your sheets,
I whispered, "I love you."
I'm sure you'd say the same to me.

What do
Men in their mid-late twenties do
For fun?
Do you have fun outside
Playing the guitar and reading?
Alone in my room,
I whisper, "I love you."
I wish I could scream it to you.

Vulnerability Olympics - Stephanie Czapla

I want to hold you
Like I'm still going to be cold in the summer,
Like there's no reason to get up earlier.
You don't need to smoke.
We don't need morning-coffee
Just like we don't need
Either of us to cook breakfast
Or make morning-coffee.

I still think about the study-questions.
Succinct queries leading to long
Conversations.
I asked you,
"What would constitute
A 'perfect' day for you?"
And you said it would start with swimming.
These days, I start my day
In your bed, or hoping to with a grin
Brimming.

Thursday on Broad and Tasker,
Three Tecates and several songs later,
I wished you were with me at the Tavern
Twirling my hands, no conversation-starters.
I wish I held you
Instead of the Tecate.
Tecate knew no fear
Except for PBRs
After Happy Hour.

I still want to hold you
From behind in my studio,
Like you're the model and my canvas.
I still want to hold you

From your fingers to your toes
So you know it's more than
Getting in your pants.
I want to hold your hands
Because I still get frightened at Rothko.
I want to hold you alone
Because Cy Twombly's Fifty Days at Iliam
Wasn't always a permanent collection.
I want to hold you close.
Morose, a feeling I want to believe is alien.
I want to hold you more
Than I feared I'd allow myself to.

I want to hold you
In conversation again,
Pick up where we left in our study-questions:
"What is your most treasured memory?"
Aware I'll retract in a week,
See,
It was when I went to a house party.
We drank, and my friend and I went swimming,
Corona Limes aside to the brim...

Retracting now as I speak,
I can't choose just one memory for this question
Except the night I swam
From Brewerytown
Down to the basement jam,
'Gansett in hand,
Ready to dance,
And we sat on the punching bag,
No touching hands.

I wanted to hold you.
I just feared getting hurt again.

(/) - Stephanie Czapla

I'll shoot crystals out of my uterus
If I'm the jeweler and purveyor.
Diamonds will fall
Granted I come on a pillar of ecstasy.
No human is entitled to this
But me.
No amount of effort by my partner
Grants them credit for my repeated
Baptisms.

Pleasure comes from within.
The epitome of pain comes forth.
The threshold of the nerves is
Penetrated by constant stimulation
Turned aberration.
"Stop it. It hurts"
Tickling is an advanced form of pain.
My legs jerk and twist as the kisses
Trickle down and numb it to
Stillness.

Sleep paralysis plagues 8% of the population.
Nearly a tenth of my pleasure comes
From physical immobilisation and
Submission.
Granting control —
Among many fetishes —
I lend a diamond from the rough
Sex is what I don't crave,
Intimacy is —
an act between
Two people —
copulating is an
Option — cuddle or

Soft speak — otherwise known as
Pillow talk —
When I'm alone, I practice kissing my
Pillow — what your lips feel nothing like because
Acupuncture on the thighs is a
Concept alien to the plush inanimate.

I'm the diamond in the rough
Sex is what I fear.
Post-come pain is
Secondary — the priority the man puts on
Pleasure — my entitlement.
Romance is the distraction.
Romantic longing correlates with sexual
Pleasure — physical satisfaction.
Symbiosis - is there such a gem without
Hurting the other?

Women grow up being told the body is a
Temple — a vengeful
Man came and shot it up.
Reclamation of blood diamonds by means of
Liberation.
Whatever that means in
Today — the lips' needles came to mind.
Crystals ready to shoot it up.

Crystals ready to shoot it up.
Diamonds in the-
Shoot it up-
Shoot it up-
Shoot it up-
I'm the jeweller and purveyor-
Shoot it up!
You're the witness and catalyst-
Shoot it up!
My pleasure is not you're doing-

Shoot it!
Diamonds in the rough sex
You found — my clit, that's impressive!
Shoot it up!
No romantic inclinations from this!
I surrender romance for primal veracity!
Diamonds in the rough
Voice!—
A noise from both crevices!
Shoot it up!
Be as violent with me as I tell you to!
I own these tears whether or not you
Shoot!
Shoot!-
....shit.

Cheeseball Olympics - Stephanie Czapla

I still think about
When you told me over
Messenger
"enjoy yr day, beautiful"
And I responded with a sticker
To trivialise the warmth in my heart
So as to not risk it freezing.

I like to switch spoons in bed
Because you're a very warm creature
And big spoons pick up more soup anyways.

Food is a joy
I learned
After letting my body starve,
And when I cook us tofu scramble,
I feel more than my anorexia recovering

You made me cry
After I came.
So much so, I told you to
Course your fingers
Up and down my sides
So I can keep my mind, body, soul, heart
Even.
Panic attack dissociation barely rivals.

When you cooked us breakfast past noon
I felt like I still should've done more
Than prep the garlic and toast.

Whenever I get sad nowadays,
Your fingers invisibly course my sides
And pull me into you,

And suddenly, I don't need another layer.
 Your lips are so soft
And I wish the alt-right didn't co-opt undercuts
Because you'd look just as hot in one
As I do in your doom metal band tee.

Cheetos are your competition
In the Cheeseball Olympics,
And I, the spectator,
Cheers for my mind, my body, and my soul,
To scrape some cheese-dust off,
Yet my heart still stays
In the lead.

You told me
You knew you were attracted to me
When we sat beside each other
On the punching bag
On the floor
At the basement show.
I knew I felt something nice about that night, too.

You asked me
If I can come over for the snowstorm.
The night of,
I came back from Poems Night
And put on Purple Rain,
Wishing you picked up your phone
So I could've walked over
And watched it with you.

The Reach - Miranda Darling

I am never out of it
my days are diarised
listed
calendarised
my every moment noted
hour productivised

I have internalised your schedule
accounted for
explained to you
justified my very f**king existence
to your spreadsheet

the tiny squares
numbers times,
haunt my dreams
stalk categorize
brain-free in sleep only
my insides look like a table
in EXCEL

my breath measured
to fill each square
in line with every
other square
measure to stack
neatly upon the
breath before

the tiny bricks
that build the day
that leave no room
for the wild roses to grow
for the heart to go hunting

for feral moments
for unruly fruits
for bitter mint
and accidental herbs

and so tile by tile
entry by entry
I am dying

not like a body collapsing
more like a soul
fracturing into pieces
small enough
to escape the mouth
with each exhalation
for each tiny particle
of everything to fly
and float it's own way
to freedom

I still cannot breathe

with every exhalation
there is more of you
and less of me

Soon you will be me

what you have ever wanted
-- to wholly posses
to inhabit to walk
to control to canniblaise
every molecule
until there is no you
no me
only you who is me

And I can't f**king stand the thought

I fought
every second
of my adolescence
to create the space
I needed to grow

I defied every iron fist
in every velvet glove

I withstood more
than I could ever
hope to survive
intact

then spent my twenties
piecing the pieces
back into the picture
spent my twenties trying
to retract
the love I had freely given

so I thought

pieces of me
pieces of you
the one indivisible whole
the one invisible hole
sunk so deep in my chest
that to fall is to fall forever

they say there is a crater in Africa
and if you fall you fall forever
and when I heard
I wondered
how long it would take

to lose the fear of falling
if you were falling forever

at first the rushing wind
awakes the terror
your guts heave up
caught in your throat
limbs in windmills
face down
face up
waiting for the crash
that will never come
-- the great correction —

how long would it take
(I wonder)
to lose the fear of falling
to accept the exception
you have been granted
from the consequences
of gravity?

would you ever?

would you ever
or does everything
given time
become normal?

does every unacceptable
thing become the thing
we now accept
as the only possible outcome?

the focus narrows

worlds shrink to marbles
horizons to tentative marks

made in pencil
hesitant sketches
raging bushfires
to sparks
that learn to extinguish themselves
and return to the dark

be where you are not
beware who you are not
for the craving
at three am
becomes the face
on the tip of the arrow
that flies to plunge
behind your eyes
so all you see
is that which you
have not
and want
so badly
you would shed your skin
and crawl naked
for as long as it took

an arrow in the soft underside
of my pink and willing cheek
drawing me
drawing me
while my fins and gills
are still within the reach

thumb in gillfold
pressing
eyes gold
with distant sunlit flame
while the reach
pulls me one way

and the barbs
of the arrow
just as stubborn
refuse to yield
and the only thing left to go
to give
is the pink and willing cheek
which tears
at last
splits my face
and with it
scars my mouth
into the semblance
of a smile

A Happier Ghost - Lillie Davidson

should she stay in her pillowed padded room
and pretend to like the shapes she has for dinner
straights and squares bending from the booze
she pours down their throats in the hope
that they'll hurl and leave early
or should she leave?
run down the curled street in worn silk slippers
yelling 'fuck you' at the two—story semi-detached shoe-
boxes
containing people she'd return if she could.
and maybe she'd rent a flat in London
like the one she had in her twenties
although a little more broken down
because rent in London is different these days
and so is she.
she's had a man on the backburner and now he can step
forward
and she's got a job in a gallery and everything is as it
should be!
but now a woman's banging on the door and waving a
ringed hand in her face
and a twenty-two year old started at the gallery and got a
promotion
and she needs that because rent in London is different
these days
but the landlady laughs when she says this and asks her
why a woman in her fifties is living like this?
boxes packed job packed in man packed up children adults
now
where to go but back down the curled street to a closed
door
and a new woman wafting through her hallways
a happier ghost for her husband to love.
no, she knows she should stay in her pillowed padded
room
curl lips at the guests she blinds with £30 moonshine
and look forward to the moment she rolls over in bed and

dies with her forehead pressed against the small of her husbands back.

Your Slender Shadow - Pauline de Drouas

The reflection of your soul dresses the lacy pearl grey paving stones
Tears rays

The city vanishes into the silver fog
Mirror of our unfinished nights

The print of your memory beads in the sleepy roofs gutters
The echo of your voice dissipates into the storm's flowers

A pool of silk washes your slender shadow
Bringing with it the debris of faded seasons
Without you the horizon sets in oblivion

Ton ombre gracile - Pauline de Drouas

Le reflet de ton âme coiffe les pavés de dentelle gris perle
Des rayons de larmes

La ville s'évanouit sous des brouillards argentés
Miroirs de nos nuits inachevées

L'empreinte de ton souvenir perle dans les gouttières des toits endormis
L'écho de ta voix se dissipe dans les fleurs de l'orage

Une flaque de soie lave ton ombre gracile
Emportant avec elle les débris des saisons fanées
Sans toi l'horizon se couche dans l'oubli

Wings of the Street - Pauline de Drouas

Angels inlaid with light
Dance of the celestial and the earthly
In the curves of dawn
Red, yellow, blue colored dreams,
Clinging to the summer syllables

Your smile draws hanging arches
Above childhood's ravines
You are looking for chunks of the sun
In the street's wings

Les ailes de la rue - Pauline de Drouas

Anges incrustés de lumière
Danse du céleste et du terrestre
dans les courbes de l'aurore
Songes colorés, rouge, jaune, bleu
agrippés aux syllabes de l'été

Ton sourire dessine des arcs suspendus
au-dessus des ravins de l'enfance
Tu cherches des morceaux de soleil
Dans les ailes de la rue

The Blue Night - Pauline de Drouas

Deep crossing of shadows
To stroll in trouble's forgotten dizziness
Remnant of a vegetal tune at the trough of the abyss
Searching for truth under the rubble of the known
Recollection of past's fawn walls
To breathe the glimmer of stars in the blue night
Winged door open towards you.

La nuit bleue - Pauline de Drouas

Traversée profonde des ombres
Cheminer dans les vertiges oubliés du trouble
Reliques d'une musique végétale au creux de l'abîme
En recherche de vérité sous les décombres du connu
Réminiscence des murs fauves du passé
Respirer la lueur des astres dans la nuit bleue
Porte ailée ouverte vers toi.

A Parade of Rose for a Ruin - Charles Derenne

Leaving from a bramble palace, where the heels will slam
no more over the marble, looking like granite.
The diamond chandeliers mourn the faces they no longer
illuminate.
The medals and beer medallions gleam their only merit.
A ballet of filth is seducing the vestiges and detritus of a
fading time.

Rebecca - Jeramy Dodds

My dolphin eats glitter for breakfast.
The jeweler's hammer of her sonar
chirps chunks off the cubic zirconia
of my hard on for her. My dolphin wolfs
glitter off A-list stars at after-after-parties
that bump till second sunrise. My dolphin
and I used to do MDMA together and pass out
our business cards to the weather.
At the Science Centre kids ask
how close we've come,
hunting down Atlantis together.
My dolphin clicks into
the hydrophone, If anything,
we've come apart. My dolphin eats
glitter to keep her figure but once
ate the forearm off a toddler
who bent in to kiss her.

Maquette for a Mall's Santa Castle - Jeramy Dodds

I hate myself as much as the rest of you
should, approaching the veal farm
and feeling peckish. I break out
in handcuffs every time I drink liqueurs.
You must not run with them, wolves
are like scalpels. The chief of all mall cops
is Santa. Santa Claws. When we eat a turkey
we also eat its shadow. Santa's castle
is an orphanage for the aborted. A haven,
where undead progeny cobble toys
for breathing children. To save on hairnets
in his delicatessen, Santa hires only
alopecians from the Appalachians.
Soap-flake snow whiter than a doll's genitals
banks against the buttresses. The parapet
roofs spin in ventilationed wind, powering
the saws in his shop. Halloween pumpkins float
in the moat, the drawbridge lined with majorettes.
Shift too much on his knee and his elvish security
hisses like balloon animals come upon
by blowguns. I don't ask for much.
Above my hammock, the sun-stroked polaroid
of Santa and I role-playing Stockholm Syndrome.
It's the polar opposite of wish. It's all I got.

Long Winter Farm — Jeramy Dodds

You've got to get to the country. The fields are empty
as if all farmhands have the clap. The trees have taken
off their fatigues, yet no one's wives rise to shoo
houseplants out for exercise. Toddlers with
twig pistols guard the cisterns, the acne-scarred planets
are light years, souffl. years, away. I've met albino elves
who harvest the guano smokebats leave in my lungs.
I suctioned a Baby On Board sign to the rear
window of a hearse. Clouds suck sun-sheen off the rocks.
I've a mound of creased choir gowns that need irony.
My favourite dog's buried in the yard. She was dead
but she got better. Now I have a Mennonite's fear
of the automobile. A raven puts on his soot and goes
to work the warmth from his algebra. Most guys in these
parts
grow a goatee even though it's cattle country. Come on
to the country, there's still seats in the nosebleeds. It's like
living
below a dam built during budget cuts, loving a geography
this much.
Why must this landscape look like luggage left unattended
in an airport to get our attention? Any resemblance
is purely reciprocal. I have an ex who's on the run in
Mexico,
or who has the runs in Mexico, or who is running Mexico,
I don't know, is her hair art or a gas-lamp mishap per-
haps?
My dog and I were like two peas in an escape pod.
When cattle rose from those valleys, cankles in frost
shackles,
I watched silent films with my eyes shut. My biggest mis-
take
was wearing white jeans to Rib Fest, but it's for fun
we waxwings set controls for the heart of the sun.

Get thee to the country. I've fletched every sparrow in this
war.
When the kill-switch sun kicks on, you can watch
lunar rogues beeline into miles of turnstile trees, trees
spilling birds like a sales force at the brink of Black Monday.
Then sucked in at dusk the way a rainbow sucks back
into an only child. Each tree the scale model of a skyproof
roof
giving up its day job. Each tree, a little town like Jonestown.
I've used a mirror to repel myself down the mountain to
these trees.
Break one's wrist and you're an arborist. Each night the
police chief
sings my alibis as lullabies to his sweet niece.
Come, come tend to me, I tend to disagree with victory.
If there were a book about Long Winter Farm
it would begin, 'A river is always too curious of its end.'

The Myth, Of Course, Is That There Will Be Some Survivors — Jeramy Dodds

ME

Of quartz I know little. Through towns
with all the charm of exit wounds,
to a clackshawed recital on your Electrolux
in the oak antechamber at Linger Farm.
Remember, if you must machete me,
run it by the whetstone first.

SHE

At dusk I entrust a dustbowl
to the doorjamb. Stooks disband
as the pressure system dovetails.
Poltergeists vie to deliver memos
to crows on gateposts in heraldic pose.
Tailwinds debrief the bowl
through its knothole.

ME

Sandhumps dune to sea, a jar
of salve for the whiplashed backs
of interned beachstones. Sun swanning
as the afterglow leans to its confidante:
'When you leave, a paparazzi of breeze
snaps me falling to my crystal knees.'

The Diorama of Our Future Breakup — Jeramy Dodds

I made a diorama of your eye exam from scratch
and sniff stickers, the colonel's favourite private
stash of weed for shrubbery. Broccolini hedges
my bets with Realism. Gallery-goers caught a rash
of suicides on their car roofs at the vernissage. Art is Art
Garfunkel's arch-nemesis. Paratroopers falling
on hard times were hired as security forces
us to be safe. If I said I had a vision I was lying
zip-tied in a sea chest. A diorama of what the carpenters
saw
in half of the magician's chests: a top hat, a hare, a cape
schooners of stolen organs couldn't round due to a raft
of shootings off the promontory. The cape I used
to get away with. I haven't jerked off since you left
the stove on. A diorama of you in tall boots and bustier
than in reality. My libertarian life coach was drawn
by pointillist horses. You and our optometrist drunk
driving
a stake through the heart of our monogamy in his mini-
van,
me beneath the marquee with the diorama I made
of your eye exam in one hand, the other waving a cake.

Boys and Bricks - Brittany Drays

The biggest mistake perhaps is that we tell daughters
that sons are made of bricks
They are strong and secure and they will protect daughters
But we fail to tell daughters that
bricks can break
And when they fall apart
They will take daughters down with them
And we fail to tell sons that it's okay to break
And we shouldn't scare sons with the weight of a woman
Sons need to know that crumbling
doesn't make them weak
But sons and daughters should be taught that they are not
weight
Meant to push over walls
Sons and daughters should take each other's bricks
And build walls together
And keep those walls
From crumbling
On each other

Cycle - Brittany Drays

I yelled at him the way my grandmother
yells at my grandfather
And there I saw
Three generations of women who don't know
how to argue out of love
But rather out of
Fear

Mothers and Sons - Brittany Drays

Your mother never touched you
That's why you touch a lot of women
And don't know what you're trying to feel
Now there is a trail of damaged women behind you
Wondering why you left so quickly
Wondering what they did wrong
Wondering why they couldn't fix you
But they couldn't fix you
They can't
You don't need to be fixed

Naked – Brittany Drays

You were the first one to see me
Completely naked
You took my guard
And slowly you pulled it down
Throwing it on the floor
You ran your warm hands along years of criticism and
never once felt it
It didn't stop you from unbuttoning my insecurities
Sliding them off my shoulders
Exposing my battle wounds that you unclasped and held so
gently
You unzipped my every flaw
That I was instructed to cover up
You stripped me of every defense mechanism that I tied
on so tightly
And there I stood
In front of you

Completely naked
Scars of a Girl – Oscar Dunbar

Because the Scars of a Girl
cause me delight
unknown but familiar
burns that excite

champagne to canapes
filled your head with sound
in the members lounge
you fell to the ground

single mother
where are your kids
lady lover
social services

down the aisle
there she goes
a brave bag of bones
her purrs echo
as mother weeps and daddy knows

Shadows crossed my path again
show me the way, Marianne
Gallows your stage in the end
show me the way, Marianne

She's an heiress of bad nature
Princess of Sin
that prays and lurks under my skin
Like clockwork I let her in

I said yes to an invitation
but you wont let me in

at their table I'll be served
just what I deserve

Shadows crossed my path
Show me the way, Marianne
Gallows your stage in the end
Show me the way, Marianne

On the Fading of the Stars — David Erdos

When one of the great voices fades
The world no longer knows how to listen;
Pictures are splintered and what was clear
In a cloud is wrenched loose.
Shining through it all is the light
That was initially formed to dare darkness;
Prising it open, like malnourished hands
On sweet fruit.

A special man has just died who I saw
Fashion light from his laughter;
A small electric bulb conjured
By the dexterous hands that wrote spells;
Dense invocations of words
And comprehensive poetics,
Erudite interrogations of the systems
And codes the failed sell.

And yet his was always success,
From early days, each endeavour;
Word photographs of the speakers
Or the stigmatics rage below stairs,
Then the spraying of truth
Across Ladbroke Grove, stars and places,
The saviour grace for the homeless
Whose continued torrent of language
Drowned out defeat and changed air.

The genius in the room with his
Fountain pen and mind water; the source
Of all rivers for those that he befriended
And loved. A man whose clear life
Captured the fog found in others,
Crystallising intention before posting to hell,

Or above. The journalist of the heart,
And Poet of the eye, whose voice music
Fused word and meaning and turned
Disasters birds into doves.

From ravens to stars he flew with all
Through his writing; Now that a new
Migration has started and we will be
Watching the sky that's now his.
We will see the perfect calligraphy
Of his lines in those streaks of dawn
And torn sunsets. Let each new thought
Now be his thought and our time with him
This life's gift.

Part of the Process — David Erdos

Part of the process of change is to recognise what is miss-
ing;
What you must do is find comfort in whatever void is left,
breach or hole.
Retract all of the fluids, instruct, and then forewarn all
successors,
That to do away with desire is to set the heart sail, uncon-
soled.

Once this is accomplished, change clothes, shave the ex-
cess hair, drink cold water.
Take down the photos, or ignore the ones scorched on the
wall.
They are merely emblems, or worse; what the past consid-
ers a medal;
The battles fought have long ended, and the blood fit to
spill has since mulled.

Now, the work starts and we must aim ourselves towards
silence,
Which is always expansive, even if at first, it narrows.
Free from the absence of fact, is the life we have left to
start over;
If you cannot remove yourself, then remember:

Once the heart has paid the price, it borrows.

Big Ugly Tattoo - Suzi Feay

At the water-park in intense July
Kids hose each other down and dare
A path through grey veils of spray,
Scamper across the moulded concrete dish
Splitting and shattering palmtree jets.
Babies sit sudden, heavy, boggled with the din.
Their skin is poignant, buttery. Blank vellum.

Every adult is a spoiled exam paper,
Rough notes towards a personality.
Everywhere I look — big ugly tattoos that announce
I want to be a dragon or a Maori or an ancient Indian
sage.
Co-ordinates. Unicorns. Skeletons playing cards.
Mums with back-fat flex rose trellises no prince will ever
climb.
Snakes coil up Krispy Kreme calves. A hot air balloon. A
swan.
You've dealt yourself a Tarot card, but it's always the same
one.
You've drilled an extravagant cutaneous vow
That you'll always feel exactly the way that you do now
But that flame whose name scrolls your breast loves some-
one else
And proof of pain's no guarantee of all the rest.

The hook of a drawn wire coat-hanger makes a pun
Of a girl's soft nape and scapular. That joke's not good
enough
To outlast the afternoon. I hope it's what it looks like,
Ballpoint pen, to be scrubbed off soon, but I'm not sure
Of anything, not least the name, sign, sigil or seal
That ever would needle outwards from my mind
To print an empty promise on my plain, changeable skin.

Romance - Sophie Fenella

Love, when we get the red wine and
suck chicken bones on dirty sofas,
when we boil a chicken carcass and
sit around a wooden box, playing
with rats, when we laugh at how
chicken skin looks like the hungover eyes
we hide behind, when we swallow
our hands chased with an extra gram
of ketamine, when we hate ourselves,
when we spit at slammed doors,
when we inject vodka on stage
as if our living room of rats and cats
was a punk concert and we are in demand,
when we soften our skin in candle light,
when we breath evaporated grease, when we
hold the last bone between us and kiss as if
our eyes are not retracting in on themselves,
when we melt words together, when we
hold our mouths open, when we fall asleep
with crystallised chalk dust and bad breath,
when we hold hands under duvets, when we
watch the sun do circus tricks,
when we are professional, when we bend over,
when we play in shower caps, when we
leave the room, when we wake up empty,
when we turn off the noise and never see
the menstruating sky play aphrodisiac
when my open legs are strung up dry.

Ghost Talk - Sophie Fenella

Almost eaten, my mother's hand -
tight-spun fist - knocks the table
as she whispers, he's here

with closed eyes and mouth
chewing baked potatoes, drowning
in butter — not enough cheese.

She is speaking to the dead.
Oh Mother, what did you do
to make this knocking sound?

Knock to keep the absent,
knock to break the door,
knock to stop the crockery
smashing on the floor.

Knock to lighten the granite air
warm the house where ghosts walk,
silence swallowed after a child leaves,
break the silence Mother,
with psychic knock.

The knock of the dead,
the damn knock of the dead,
is the reason my mother
worries the lonely wall,

when the kitchen table
is a great big apology
and we sit chewing carbs.

There is no reason why
my mother knocks rustic tables

like a priest in fables
or deeper stories than this.

And there is no explanation why
I feel my witch blood boil
with the sound of the knocking dead.

The most important moment
of healing is the bit when
the ghost becomes personable.

My mother watched the ghost walk
through the kitchen, as arguments
widened her eyes and for the first time

I saw her as a child
brushing soft palms
on my five year old brow.

Neither of us could explain why
the hallway rocked when the ghost
turned up in the kitchen
with his hairy arms, orchestral laugh,
and meditative smile.

Faultlines - John Finnigan

It's been raining cats and dogs
On one side of the street.
The street itself is a river
That seized-up after complications.

What became The North Encampment
Was chosen by The Umbrellas
While The Parasols went South.
Two peoples divided by a stiff course.

Or is it a division of hemispheres?
One brain one world two divisions?
Montagues. Capulets. Jets. Sharks.
Parasols. Umbrellas. When is a parasol

An umbrella? Only the Sphinx knows!
In the local slammer there's a permanent
DMZ which Parasols and Umbrellas alike honour.
When is a river not a river? asks Parasol

Pete. When is a door not a door? queries
Umbrella Bob. Desert Island Discs is playing
In an adjacent cell. The disc that
The multi-billionaire is choosing

To rescue from the waves is I'm
Walking Backwards For Christmas.
The Sphinx is his luxury. The Bird that could stand
Much Reality tweets then double-takes.

Jade Angeles Fitton - Orchestra of Pylons

I miss the pace, if I'm honest. If I'm honest,
I miss making margaritas braless behind the bar, with my
lost friends egging me on, I miss lacking class.
I miss cracking glass, slapping tarts, watching boys brawl,
crashing through walls. I miss creating new scars.
I miss the race, I want excess, I miss the tumble, I like dis-
grace. I find romance in it.
I crave attention, I like aggression. Can I entice you to
fight me?
I'm born the year of the tiger, I like to be cornered.
Come a touch closer,
I'll be the pain you've been pining ...

I miss the pace, if I'm honest. If I'm honest,
I miss your name in my mouth, like a sweet I roll around.
I miss crying wolf. I hate standing tall. I like being chased,
but what I love's
getting caught. I like bratty, I like bitchy, I like catty, I like
spoilt.
I like smashing tennis balls in to the other court.
I miss dancing. I miss shouting. I miss big. I miss grand. I
miss the West of
America, I miss all my worst plans.
I miss carelessness, recklessness, the mottling of flesh. I
miss the clamp of fear that held me together, kept in my
mess.

I miss the game, if I'm honest. If I'm honest,
I miss being run through the mill. I even miss dead blue-
bottles on the windowsill.
Still, I'm nimble from my childhood years; and still,
there's the thick, soft grass I'd jealously watch the horses
eat,
there's still rivers and streams, the nettles still sting.

But now there's never a sound but the wind, that howl.
That pain between the wires, an orchestra of pylons, just to remind me
I miss the streets. I miss the hard concrete that once fractured my teeth.
I repeat: if I'm honest, I miss the pace.
So my advice is chase only the heat, and revel in it.

Her Faceless Glory — Maria Gazis

Her faceless glory
put me on my knees,
the holiness of her
affected my wholeness
in a way it never had before

The way she tends to push you
but sometimes stop and wait
connects us all
in this cosmos of
runners and crawlers
and those who seem forever paused

My Softness — Maria Gazis

My softness is not a threat
against your armour
of shame
and masculinity faked

I am here
with all I am
which is all I'll ever need
to push against your (un)kind

My softness,
your fragile ways;
somebody might say
we are alike
but there is nothing alike about
my fragility which makes me strong
when yours

makes you sad, unable to plead
or bleed

My softness
is the ultimate armour

Brighton - Frankie Glace

Melting between the blue   I see
sky meets sea   I speak
whisper then howl.
Still.
Before it jumps to its feet in applause
clapping the pebbled ground and enveloping our steel
skeleton.
Our hearts laid out to rest, out West.
Touching my toes, it moves my feet
I hear it in my sleep, it out reaches my reach
darted looks, scrambling in flight
It's too deep   to stay
I leave with salty skin
salty cheeks.
The blue   I see
where the sky meets the sea
never has a goodbye been so sweet.

Soup — Salena Godden

Imagine if seven people from seven nationalities
Came to your home to share one pot of soup
You would have seven conflicting versions of that soup
Someone would write to note the flavour. Another the
heat
Someone would write about the meaning of soup
The size of the portions. The memory the soup triggers
Too salty. Not enough meat.
This is a stew? It's more a casserole!
This soup is a meal in itself!
I'm gluten intolerant!
The hungriest person at the table would just write: Thank
you
This is human nature –
We look around the table and
Examine the world just as we do these dinner guests
We note our differences
Skin and manners, clothes and language
And we forget to sing
We forget to celebrate that we are one
That the act of love was the sitting down together
And sharing the pot of soup in the first place
And we say nothing
As they put someone in prison for using a fork to eat their
soup
We silence the person that slurps soup from the bowl
And we ignore all the women because…
What the fuck does a woman know about soup anyway?
Some sit around the table and demand bread with their
soup
Others feel entitled to the whole pot of soup … all for
them
And there's always someone who will piss in the soup
So the soup is ruined for everyone

And sadly this is all human nature too
I'm too sad to finish this poem about soup
I'll just say
I have so much to be grateful for
I'm so lucky
I have a warm kitchen
A pot and some vegetables
Today I'm gonna make time
Today I'm gonna make love
Today I'm gonna make soup
Fuck war!
Make love!
Make soup!

A MAN ON THE RADIO WHO IS
TRYING NOT TO BE IN A GANG SAYS

the
right
feels
like
the
wrong
and
the
wrong
feels
like
the
right
just now
you know?

AND HE IS CRYING AND NOW I
UNDERSTAND THE TRAP A LITTLE MORE.

Losian - Sinead Graham

I've walked myself somewhere but I don't know how I got
here
If you asked me to trace the path out in thin air,
I'd point everywhere,
I'd go in circles until I made a whirlwind
May the world spin
on even when we're lost and lonely
And the parts of us are too scattered to pick up so we only
hold on to what we think we're worth
That's why I dropped you
And I bet it hurt but that pain can't get through
I'm already full
Hating myself and hating the earth
And hating that I hate them too.

Cinderella - Lily Guy-Vogel

Once upon a time in some far away flats
There lived a young woman with two little brats
With no one to help she was rushed off her feet
Working two shitty jobs just to make ends meet
Each evening was spent in tedious housework
She cursed her ex-boyfriend — the selfish jerk
In battle against the sea of crap on the floor
Her life was chore after chore after chore
Eating cold spaghetti hoops with a large glass of red
She sits head in her hands before going to bed

And after all that she did were her kids grateful?
Like fuck! They were perfectly totally hateful
Of course she absolutely loved them to bits
But they were a right little pair of moany shits
She dreamed of escape for a day or a night
Surely to some fun she still had a right?

On an especially horrible, difficult day
When her boss was a dick and the sky was grey
When the kids wouldn't eat but played with their food
And the guy on tinder sent an unwanted nude
Cindy sat on the sofa and picked up her phone
And saw something that made her instantly groan
In tears she sat and gave a little wail
Her friends got Glastonbury tickets in the resale

Two Untitled Poems - Svetlana Grishina

1.

Again I don't know how to sleep
And birdsong bores through glass of windows
And white rectangles:
Of the screen, the ceiling, cigarette-pack
And shivers take roots right into my back
Undressing me to tender nerves
Depriving me of boundaries and form
And rain is hanging from the sky
And walls - as lack of them
And the floor as The Path
The calendar- blank pages
Of light thoughtlessness
I overtighten clockface with a strap
Transforming even circle to infinity of number eight
Having forgotten names and places
And, having switched a chisel for a flute,
I'm waiting for the world to enter thought.

2.

Under the microscope of my window,
In section:
Humidity
That leaves chrysalis of salted water on faces
Then
Will be born
A butterfly of flittering eyelashes:
A blitz life,
Hardly for an hour.
The evil
Yellow smell of London

Dives, like an animal,
Into the hole of window frames
Plays with the ball
Of nerves
Scratches leather lining of veins
With a chiselled claw of melancholy
A domestic
Hellhound.
I am starting to sprout with wildflowers
Of redolent dreams
And vacuous blindspots
And the weed of blissful laze
This spring is here to stay and last
Across the whole of expanded desert of me.

The Remains - Regina Gunapranata

What remains after nothing?
A great expanse of earth, of stardust?
More nothingness?

I've discovered what remains is this:
Brutal Desire.

Sky, moon, sun, earth:
You are the sky
and I am bare earth underneath you.

Your horizon grazes
the highest peaks of my mountains,
skimming—till blue in the face—
almost touching.
Your clouds caressing softly,
softly, the jagged peaks of my being.

Desire for you is so strong:
The waters in my oceans crash into each other,
Tsunamis as tall as skyscrapers...
But they're never built tall enough...
Erected just so:
always aiming to graze
the hem of your atmosphere.

I am earth, and you are sky
so the waters of my being dissolve
into you
my furthest most reach evaporates
into droplets and then,
nothingness.

And yet I do know this:

I am made of you,
and you of me.
The particles from me,
evanesce in you,
I dissolve into your being,
the same way your being dissolves
into mine;
a shoreless sea of non-beings.

The Delta - Regina Gunapranata

Lay your claim on me:
upon my delta let your soft sails graze,
feel the wet of the water, it is river, it is sea.
Let my waves break over the oak of your ship;
perhaps I will make the wood grow to bend, to stiffen, to
sing

What kind of song can the oak in wet sea sing?

Lay your claim on me asks the oak to the sea
The sea, the river, the land will open and urge your heav-
ing masts forward
forward
forward once more
till the oak in the sea breaks forth,
its treasures:
white pearls spilling upon verdant valleys

The delta sighing,
at last,
you've laid your claim on me.

Deep Ocean - Regina Gunapranata

Then slowly,
as the late spring in Paris,
the wettest spring,
the verdant waters
of the Seine inching above barriers
to caress the burning cement sidewalks
the flood turning the city lush and green
as the buds of flowers
as the leaves of trees
bloomed,
so did we.

and like the lovers in poems of long ago:
You loved me deep ocean,
I loved You deep ocean.

We dove and dove,
deep into ocean floors—
seeing blue, seeing You,
seeing You, seeing blue;
always depth for depth.

You came into my life
gently, gently,
lapping into the shores
of my past, present, future.

They say water erodes rock,
rock turns to sand,
sand fills the shores of my life,
shores upon which
your water
laps, laps, laps.

You, deep ocean
You, come into my life
gently gently,
lapping into the shores
of my past present future

i, dove in, deep ocean—
not knowing how to swim.

Dream Children - Charlotte Hanger

Do you remember the lemon blowy daffodils?
They wandered lovely in a silent dream like children high
on love and mirrorshine and birds fluttering on drink
and lust
Their autumn voices lit the tea crowds like vintage soaks in
a milky lake after dusk while little fools lay beneath grand
domes
Lazy art could sing sweet once
It could fly them to wise time and falling grass
Let all be cold
To the floating happy dew garden they crept,
A secret silver garden that could carry a white sky where
riddles twinkle at witches' hour
And all behind a moon spangled heaven
Where to triumph they need only slow dancing in the rain
and golden glitter in their hair
And who did night despair of?
Not them by far
Please swim far away from my cold red heart
It said
And they said

We write for thread and you
Come lie here softly because we have seen that paradise is
nothing but beautiful diamonds
Let's marry summer

You Are - Charlotte Hanger

The unwanted ghost that haunts yesternight
That exorcism didn't work out then
The vapour in my old perfume beads
I've got a new one by the way it's in a dark green bottle
with a gold lid and it doesn't smell of you
The aftertaste of those scallops in balsamic vinegar from
the market
A shadow that trips with every wind song
Nowhere yet everywhere
That fox that cries like a banshee outside my window every
bloody night
A small attic at the top of the new house filled with mem-
ories not to be treasured
- don't open those
The Darling Letters
Isn't that what Carol called them?
Some darling
Baby, teddy, moo...
Absurdity now
Unseen unheard unexisted
Your skin cold at the touch
Throw me the shovel
And I will plant
at your grave

For Sale - Charlotte Hanger

Roll up roll up for the Primrose Hill tours
Where I found my heart and you found yours

By Adelaide Road that sunny paved street
Where poets write and lovers meet

In the Russian tea rooms or that blue bookshop on the
green
Blue plaques galore London's literary dream

Sylvia first came here with the golden leaves
Full of joy in Autumn, still she breathes

But this was our story too not just her and Hughes
Roll up roll up please form orderly queues

To see the small dogs jumping on their leads
The gemstone makers and their glittering beads

That candled Greek restaurant I forget its name
I wonder now would it taste the same

Tickets torn in two, tour's over now
Ladies and gentlemen please take a bow

As the curtain closes on another day
More memories sold I wonder what you'd say

Today is - Alastair Hodgen

Today is
Bumblebee Tuesday he announces
As he rolls up his sleeve
-A tattoo for everyday of the week.
Where can I get batteries?
I'm thinking those recycling bins in supermarkets.
A Hare Krishna asks which way the drums went.
Not sure so we send him over there with a wave
Of the hand that happens to be into the sun.
Someone asks directions to the simple street theatre.
It's a low wooden box structure with a handrail.
Two actors.
A pair of fools.
One describes his favourite building
All the brown brick of a train station
Where he tried to take his life.
Act two and they're invisible. In love.
Converts. Committed to the project.
The crowd pummel them with foodstuffs and leave as it
gets dark.
In the hubbub one of them kicks over the fools' money
box
coins are sent rolling every which way and slippered feet
dart out
like little dams to stop the small silver change trickling
away.
Today is Wednesday
The radio drama continues,
His voice resonating authority —
"I thought he was dead. It's hard,
I couldn't tell anyone. I told you that night
I threatened to kill you, remember?
-Sweat appears on his face-
He was in prison for years in Pakistan,

One in Afghanistan, just got out and
Holed up in Sweden.
I was intimidated, wow. Everything
You did even the digital stuff. All good,
Seriously, stuff you can do now"
The radio ceases.
Buckles give way
She looks deep into my eye,
Deep as I imagine it looks myself,
It was like bouncing round a curved wall before she
grabbed my forearm took me aside
And asked what the hell I was doing.
I could only justify myself in rebellion,
Made sure to spit on what we stood on.
It's so easy to get swept up in it all,
First night stand up. Make a point.
Thursday night
Cheeks overfull with food and the colour pink.
A collision with the road surface.
Your new found power,
Slightly softer soil,
Feet trampling down,
The ancient tree where the roots can't breathe.
Palm flat smack outstretched on a pane of glass
Shut into a coffee shop leading up the arm,
Elbow, robe full of colours and a mystic's beard
And the eyes of a seer up a rigid neck
And his head is wearing a tall cone shaped hat like a
dunce,
And you can see the café dwellers really think
'now here is someone not like us'.
Arm in arm we leave the house
With the joy of empty pockets
But a blood pact to be doubly prepared tomorrow
And full of the joy of independence
Or at least the illusion
And a taste for chimera.

All day Friday
A loose bicycle bell jingles at every bump,
Pleasantly,
People turn to look at it,
The bell is carried from one end of the city to the other.
Everything is still there.
Two friends are making dry point prints from juice cartons,
Remembered colour in black and white,
They invent images.
A far cry, thrown across the flat night landscape with a
Strip of light and vague olive sky.
Your mouth shut tight refusing to speak,
Unless I find your natural resonance,
So I start humming.
You sing me Mel's cockney songs,
And draw me a primrose
And I tell you about crossed letters.
One day someone will lift off your guilt
Like a cloak and you won't believe
You ever went out wearing it.
Until then I will only love you
With an efficient love, waited for and found,
Caught in throat song,
Purged of tremendous gaping lust
Moments submitted to nothing.
She says —play the lowest note on the piano
And then don't come back to me.
Complain into the pit of the neck,
That it's not as pretty as cupid's bow.
Watch an anatomist love the body of an old man,
And grin salacious over the belly dancers in Turkey.
Feet in his handkerchief
Finger-tips. The sunlight.

Sentinel Haiku - Vanessa Vie and Michael Horovitz

On the lookout post

Atop the fishmonger's van

— A single seagull

Accordion Haiku — Vanessa Vie

Sound of an accordion

Flying above the railway

— Shadow of a crow

John Cage Nachtmusik — Michael Horovitz

Youths spatter big noise

 revving engines hours on end

— Sweet dreams sent packing

Once Again a Wolf — Julia Houghton

At first you would come fresh from the hunt.
Jaws salivating as you greedily devoured my
mouth, that was also untamed,
vicious and only uttered agreeable grunts.

We would rip our pray apart.
Fight to be the first to reach the inners
and feast upon moist flesh,
an ever pleasant task.

When the feast was over,
the pray devoured,
We would lick each other's wounds and lay,
lazily side by side,
empowered by our display.

We would howl wildly at the moon.
A warning to other wolves that the territory we roamed
had now been claimed.
You would take me, mate me,
Knowing not if my mind or body approved.

The feeling of the way we once came together in a time
when youth was new.
Our canine instincts raw,
untamed.

Then one spring our pups were born.
A nearby tribe would throw us scraps.
These morsels then replaced the hunt due to convenience
and reliability.

Now I look upon our wild days and lament.
With time we have become a well tamed dog.

Those wolves are well bread out.

We sit by fire light and rest our worn worked bodies.
In a house that we don't own.
We converse and eat at well positioned intervals.
The pray is now served cooked without the bones.

There is no untamed howling,
we have no reason to warn other dogs away.
We are neutered terriers that lead a happy life.
Well fed, well loved and walked each day.
A stroll with leads and collars to a park with a playground
and gates.

But sometimes, when the owners are away,
in your eyes I can't mistake that look of rabid wolf that has
took the doggies place.
I growl, you groan and to our long forgotten cave we
wolves still go.
To feed on memories and feast upon those thoughts.

Ode to the Orgasm – Julia Houghton

I lay restless in the dark tresses of your cuckoo
brown
hair.
Where madness met metaphysical memory momentarily.
The clouds covered the sky like a blanket of broth.

There two, so called souls,
sat
situated
upon each other.
Locked rigid in natures
nutritious
embrace,
embarrassed.
Harassed moments, only just passed,
since we were uncovered,
unashamed.

Untamed nudity tells the truth,
Climaxing temperatures lie not.
Hot in the millisecond of clarity that adorns the mind
with sweet temptation.

Standing
stagnant
swaying slightly,
to a beat that still rings in our hips.
Lips dry with pure sticky moisture,
that is light and unseen.

Unclean bodies sweat sweet dews
that smell of guilt and of pleasure.
Measured by passersby who know also the scent of the act.

They smirk and react in accordance to that fact.

Drawing visions of the art in one's heart.
Primal
Pictures
Pulsating.
Relating to all that is life
in that one second of empty
thought.

A divine act divided
by safety and caution.
Reminded of an instinct
that could fraught all survival,
If rivalled by the means of mankind.

Drink juices that quench thirst,
as some just help dehydrate.
Shapes shake to become violent and radiant all at once.

Discipline is unwelcome
unless called in a code word,
Or screamed from the throat
Like a screech made by caged hawks.

Talk on cream pillows
with pink rose buds sewn on
and whisper never ending,
Unrealistic nothings
Into ears that still ring.

Tingling tapestries
are weaved around our lies,
Laying unjustifiably refined.
Behind the grunts of giving,
Receiving is also gift that grants gracious groans given
meaning.

Revealing a language that changes
each embrace,
laced with a feeling of mutual taste.
Waste not a tear drop
that falls from the eye,
like a pear placed precariously
upon a plate.
Or wait for the water and soft tissue to surface and wipe
what's not wanted away.

Then dream sweet of illicit incantation,
that would in the past,
have been burnt by strict flames.

Arise from that state in a glow of amusement,
no shame,
not a trace.
Because lust often brings
welcome deep purple darkness
to the lingering luminous light.

The sun has its mornings.
The moon has its nights.
But at times they can both share the sky.

Blossom - Rosalind Jana

Daytime, and you are confetti perfect:
miraculous in your pink and white froth.
You show off, spring bride, ever the midst
of attention as you linger on streets,
drape yourself against church walls.

Each morning you wait, ready for an audience.
Plenty stop - holding out their phones -
but these offerings are not yours to keep.
They take, take, take
and move along.

But I have seen you after dark,
a stranger creature. Especially you,
magnolia, that usual blush —
elegant gradation of colour —
made pale.

To compare you to Havisham would be too neat.
You are not forgotten, nor skeletal.

Instead, you regain yourself in gloom,
only half-seen,
nigh on impossible to capture.
As I pass you, stretching over
the pavement, I know
this is more intimate:
almost trespass.

You do not mind.

In fact, you loose a gust of blossom
smell, fresh and sweet at 10pm,
to send me on my way.

Spines — Rosalind Jana

(1)

They stretch —
neverending, gently curving,
a bright serpent of vertebrae
on the motorway.
I think this every time I see
them, how the lamps,
with their two heads, their
regimented place and length, resemble
some strangely flexible backbone.
I don't think this is what Woolf
meant when she talked of things
"lit, half-way down the spine" -
designating the soul's seat
somewhere beneath the shoulder
blades. Still, they stand arranged
like bones — steady, glowing,
dependable as they hold
the road in place
each night,
each day.

(2)

But then again, I see spines everywhere.
Branches, rail-tracks, the ridge of hills.
I've no interest in the straight ones.
Why would I? Instead it's the twists,
the shifts, the rise and fall
of lines; curvature
wherever I can find some
unlikely mirror for mine.

Lights — Rosalind Jana

(1)

They stretch —
neverending, gently curving,
a bright serpent of vertebrae
on the motorway.
I think this every time I see
them, how the lamps,
with their two heads, their
regimented place and length, resemble
some strangely flexible backbone.
I don't think this is what Woolf
meant when she talked of things
"lit, half-way down the spine" -
designating the soul's seat
somewhere beneath the shoulder
blades. Still, they stand arranged
like bones — steady, glowing,
dependable as they hold
the road in place
each night,
each day.

(2)

But then again, I see spines everywhere.
Branches, rail-tracks, the ridge of hills.
I've no interest in the straight ones.
Why would I? Instead it's the twists,
the shifts, the rise and fall
of lines; curvature
wherever I can find some
unlikely mirror for mine.

Full Moon – Rosalind Jana

The moon is a bitch.
And she knows it. Look at her!
Smug and round, stretched
to a heavy, milky girth.
Don't think she's just a fair
silver maiden, a metaphor
for you to put to use, some
shining beacon whose very
presence illuminates your verse.
She's not a lantern, a goddess,
a virgin. Don't mention Artemis,
or any other mythology.
All she's fertile with is mischief.

The moon's a bitch.
Trust me on this.
Bright malevolence – that's her.
When full, straddling the sky,
she's unstoppable. Oh she might
hide between trees, peer out
carefully from behind the
phone mast at the top of the hill,
but don't be fooled.
Nothing gets in her way.
I don't know how she does it –
exerting chaos from on high,
amplifying nerves and tears -
but she does.

The moon's a bitch!
See the way she puts people
on edge. Some weep. Others
bicker, stay out of sorts –
irritable for unknown reasons.

She twitches the strings,
mistress of small grievances
and needless arguments.
For those of us who know her moods,
accidents happen, hard words are
exchanged, sleep broken
as we toss and turn
beneath her ripened reign:
waiting for the bitch to wane.

EUROPE, AFTER THE RAIN — Miranda Keyes

DON QUIXOTE
MR POTATO HEAD
DUSK RIDING
SIDE
SADDLES
PORCELAIN HEADED

THE WEATHER IS TURNING
GREY
MOIST
PURPLE PIGEONS ON THE SEA FLOOR

TO BEND

CARS LIKE FISH
FISH LIKE CARS

FAST PIGEON IN TROPICAL RAIN HUM

DOWNTOWN MILKY BAPTISM

AT SOFT INTERSECTION

WRIST BLASTING

IN SILVER GRAPE CLIP GARDEN
ORANGE SLUG – LIKE WATER BUFFALO
MOVES IN WET FURROW

IT'S RAINING IN SOHO

1994 - Louise King

I came from a broken home
Single parent coupon home
Down the red brick DSS
I collect my labels
Council class, free school meals
The miss fit bit at the end of the road
Beside the sea at the end of the world

Around the corner-school and friends
Who would kit me out in charity shop culture
Big words and stolen beliefs
Taken from the NME and the next big thing
To take over our lives

No cigarettes today
Still scrimping for the ski trip
I hardly think so
Go along to their stand alone homes
To breathe in back garden barbecues
And family sized collections of qualifications and memo-
ries

Crawl out under parkers
From last night's party
And trundle home in Oxfam corduroy
To teacher mothers and artist fathers
I'll get back to pretend professional life
All nice and snug in my benefit bohemia

Like minded mindlessness
Kept us together longer than expected
Trying to do each other over in alternative ratings
Running from all common and conformed
Think what would have happened if we hadn't happened?
    Thank God

Elliott - Lara Konrad

I don't know why I thought you were the most handsome
man I had ever seen. Your careless frame and that smallest
face.
Slipping back and forth between those dirty aisles of the
deli,
looking for cash and other purposes

that always end
somewhere, somehow.
You saw me and you wanted me. Partially because bound-
aries don't exist
when we're young and memoryless and anything. That late
afternoon,
how we temporarily changed each other's lives standing at
the freezer section, searching for skim milk and eggs that
weren't broken.
How everything behind us just kept melting,
all that fruit, all those people,
I think about that, and how falling
in love,
at its very threshold, perhaps somewhere closer,
must be the moment where we most exist, deliberately.
Blood rushing
more lonesome and hungry.
An empty country, babe , but thriving.
You were the first one I learned to admire,
a decade later I still search you
in the future of all these men
who are more handsome but exhaustible but whole
and sinking differently.
The way I still wake some of these mornings
escaping inside memory.

When we laid in your bed,
above us the highest of ceilings,
how you wanted to listen to the same story
all over.
How as a child I once burned my feet
in the sand of Greece
and how because of the village bursting into flames
we slept on the beach that night. And how it's still the ice-
cream I remember most, vanilla dripping down my knees
while they rushed
to the house to the car.
And how I couldn't hear the ocean.
Whenever you asked a question,
expectations, yours and others' too,
became entire worlds. Softer.
You were human, and endless
to me.

Three Poems — Elena Larrson

(8)

                Daytime — I don't feel right
if i haven't been outside.   when it's light everyday —
Yes.   it's a way absolutely everyone can express
themselves; it can be a seduction, can be art, be comfort.

        I find myself switching off, the words
not my own. Into a blue dawn, everyday, she rises :
                    separate yet together
                    Serendipity, he says
surrounded with —
who knows. these thoughts sit silent ; . Love —
covered in butter

(22)

the night is the best time to be alive .

Even if the warm significance of you

is quick to slip
from my sight .

(2)

My love sits
        & holds you in its arms.

until there's nothing to say, except —
romance is futile.
& I'm sorry for leaving

i'm sorry for leaving, again and again.
Nothing, you said, was accidental

      Yet i sit in the shade of believing,
      And sometimes, sand

      falls through the cracks.
      Even when it's meant to be

held above the water

When the Wind Blows the Water White and Black (Prufrock at War) – Mathilde Leblond

The white frothy cavalry endlessly
charges forth atop the waves,
never quite reaching its destination.

Time after time its exploding sound
announces the start of a new war
never to be waged.
(Unfinished business which was never
meant to be shared.)

Born in an impossible resounding
boom, it storms then fizzles
out before reaching its destination.

And the shore, constantly under attack,
endlessly awaits the bloody battle –
to bring it some relief,
to perhaps end it all.

Still, the cavalry keeps rushing forth
But is defeated by habituation.

There shall be no conclusion –

People will get used to just about
Anything.

Don't have a title for this one yet — Jamie Lee

i want to touch your lips with someone else's hands
and then shoot you in the mouth
with a high calibre revolver
have you laugh with me in our bed one last time in a
dream
see you eat red meat with a knife
i want you condemn death and all global free market trade
the exodus from egypt, the tribes of the americas,
the reformation of the church and modern art can all go
straight to hell!
I want to see your face in a synthetic hospital light
holding a child
and cry at abrahm lincoln's death
and cry at my death
and shoot abraham lincoln
and shoot the coffin
with us in it
I want you to cry for the holocaust and for the homeless
i want to see you laughing at another man's joke at a party
i want to see you getting lost in supermarkets
and committing road rage in your pyjamas
i want world leaders to recognise your sense of comic tim-
ing
and for you to become a pitiful success in the art world
i want you to feel pain that is never-ending
i never want you to lose your working class anger
and please, i beg you, continue to hate my grandmother
and would you mind if you walked with a limp?

i also wouldn't mind seeing you being fucked by
a dog
and swim naked with an alligator
i would like you to be a mathematics genius
i would like to see you dress as a man

with a red bowtie and a whip
i would like to see you shoot a gun at a policeman
and run into my arms
i would like you to be a hospital
and ban death, poverty, cruelty and ignorance and adidas
trainers
i would like you to be spain's rail network system
so i can ride inside you
to be john nash
john macenroe
be half past seven
my first drink
a snapped shoelace
an orgasm in a toilet cubicle on top of a mountain
and a small oceanic fish
because you would make them all look so ridiculous
i want you to enjoy pornography

i want you to let me wash you, sponge you and then towel
you down in your new boyfriend's bathroom
while i compose the most exquisite music, imitating Bee-
thoven
i want you to watch me towelling us down while the light
flickers
i want to hold a door open for you and shout at a plane
and blow cigarette smoke on the moon for you
i want to hold your hand in the hospital again
i want you to forgive me for leaving you there to die

i would not like you have a breakdown at fifty after three
kids and 3 husbands and a sense of tremendous failure
i would not like you to feel pain that is never-ending
and i never want to see you work in a cafe ever again
or be alone at a funeral
or step on paving those stones that splash water up into
your shoes
i do not wish for you to shit yourself

i wish you had never done anything that you hadn't done
i wish you had had drug fuelled sex in cars with sad boys of
the north
i wish you had an exboyfriend whose cock was bigger than
mine
i wish you had seen lancashire reservoir sunsets that lasted
until it was time for tea
i wish you had stood up to your mother at 5 years old
watching her leave for the last time your fists on your hips
and a frown of ages
i wish you had left blackburn for university and a life in
the arts
i wish you had made great posters for art school damning
them all
i wish you loved your father too much
i wish your hands were hard, the fingers tapering out like
a starfish
I wish you wrinkle your nose when you laugh
and look extremely ugly in the way i pretend to admire
i wish you walk like a king of a country you created
i wish you talk behind my back
i wish you ridicule me in front of your friends
i wish you fucked sam after the funeral
i wish you cowardly forsake me
i wish you rise in the morning and tell yourself you do not
care
i wish you call me 'home'
i wish you lie
i wish you were only nice to me when you are high
i wish you leave me

i wish you paint me anyway you want
i wish you with a new human man

in a council estate in blackburn where the wild winds are
and the noise of your drowning race is strong

tell me, now who is going to to inspect the state of the
blackheads on your nose
and how your skin smells and to know that your feet
are still small and your skin very soft
and your flesh firm and your mouth still shaped like a
boat
and you're working for us to summarise each other

our love was something rancid, really,
and banal as a row of suburban gardens
and as i love the south london train line to your house

and real couples, i mean they stick it...to the death-heat
dont break when things get hard
through rehab through alcoholism through infidelity
and madness and depression and a failed suicide attempt

i want you to know that you can bore me
i want you to know that i have never shared a bed with
someone
before and enjoyed it so much - our sleep-bodies match
i want you to know i think you are a profound hypocrite
you have a pathological inability to admit when you're
wrong
i love you for it
i want you to know that i stayed with you because
you give exceptional blowjobs
and because i decided to love you and never leave you
against my better judgement
i want you to know that i find other people excruciatingly
awful
in comparison with your good aspects
i want you to know that you are flawed and i am a drug
that keeps you from examining yourself
i want you to know you are perfect
i want you to know i am a poor judge of perfection
i want you to know that its ok to defecate

i want you to know that i dont have to love you

i want you to know your art needs work
and you have been completely governed by your friends
i would like you to know i do not think
you are capable of this level of kindness
and that's ok – you will inevitably use this against me
it's what you have to do to say goodbye

i want you to know that i fear what you are capable of
and that you should learn how to cook

i want you to know that when you hear thunder
it means im having sex with someone else
and if you ever trip on an escalator to the tube
that im thinking about marrying a waitress
i want you to forget me
i want you to eat pizza and forget me
i want you to fuck, i love you fucking
i want you to be happy without me
im going to take responsibility for your future happiness
it's the only way i can see through this mist, this thinking
all about your red body
can't you see this is just my way of saying goodbye?

i want to watch you play a synthesiser in a green suit
and know that part of my fear of loving you
was the fear that one day i would have to watch you die

you are a good person within limits
you are mad and far too conservative
you do not know who you are

I want you to know that I am not a shadow
That I am contrary, humourless and not a poet
I want you to know I enjoyed being away from you at social
functions

Especially in the company of the opposite sex
I want you to know that if you say any different
You are a liar

i want you to know that if i am hit by a car i will see your
face
and feel very angry about it

I want you to know with each line of this poem I write I
love you a little less
I want you to know that children are being murdered by
jet planes in Syria
By pilots who have children and may or may not be vaguely
homosexual
and that flowers grow sweet on the hillsides of scotland
and i have watched ponds, and visited the devil, and felt
true suffering at your leaving
I want you to know I cannot separate you from the world
or me

i want you to read this poem

i want you to know that this is a spell to help you reappear
it isn't working

i want you to know that im not going to mention those
ludicrous pictures
that you post online in your underwear
and im not going to mention how perhaps this is just a
way of me posting pictures of myself
online in my underwear
you are a fool
i am a fool
the difference is is that i can admit it

(i know you will turn to sex to take revenge on my memory

i will turn to love to take revenge on your soul)

the way you take me into your mouth like a heartswell
you are a fool of specific proportions
yu are still that child standing up to your mother and you
have not left that moment
you confuse strength with brashness
you confuse bravery with cruelty
you should read more books
examine your own mind
love someone else
go back home to blackburn
forgive your mother
stop loving your father
come home, tell me what to do with these poems
forgive us,
you are still the child that walks the dead night
hoping for a mother to rescue her from the winds and
horror of your own birth
i am not that mother
no one will be
forgive me
for not trying harder.

Here's to the dead boys and the laughing prayer — Jamie Lee

in the bar again - hanging over it in a long coat
i mumble the words of old poems through beer reeking
breath
to the chorus of the chatter of old men,
the high-pitch staccato laughter of the girls
and the rolling drone of talk;
a perfect music to me now
that i am death

inexpressible thoughts of universe shine in me:
like
what is love now that death has seized its reign?
and
how to arrange
this trash of phrases like a painter
heretic to our religion of noise

my sick symphony
drowns the protests of this audience;
my coughing brothers
lost on a ship
regarding
the final sanity
as an animal madness;
our sole human fact.
gods and bestial
alike as each.

to us drinkers,
life is just 'strange'

as i twitch from left to right
admiring the twenty-something at the end of the bar

a black choker around her neck
summoning the young male staff in flashy gear
that hang like fruit on her cheap words - imagining
the way she fucks
and whose round it is,
in the madness of their youths

(i see her, poor wretch, making all
the same mistakes as i did.)

and in the corner, an old smirking saint sits; staring
through the centuries
with wet-wild eyes a pair of brilliant diamonds shot into
his face; gleaming with tears
shopping bag on the table
two straws in his pint
and
without her

the pub; our english stage of banal desperations; frozen as
a painting;
suspended in our purgatorial dream between monsters;
the men commit themselves to the altar of now!
with each sip an insidious prayer, a goodbye! to the ter-
rible pasts;
a waving off of life as if it were a pesky fly
and drink it away
as
i do

and it's seeing this - wet lipped, that
as i glimpse the impossibility of any reasonable truth
the laughing prayer begins in my stomach
and taking my last portion of lover to drink him;
whisper a new madness to myself;

"holy are my manias!

holy are my dreams of perfect life!
holy are my drinks!
holy are my smoke lungs!
holy are us unholy!
holy the girl on the end!
holy the man with the wet wild eyes!
holy are my deaths!"

and putting down my empty glass

"here's to us boys! to the all day all night boys!
here's to the dead boys!"

and
leave the bar
head bowed to the blessing rain:

a devil
singing to himself.

and
waking up

find heaven
and hell
in the same note.

heaven: love and peace upon the earth
and hell: alone in the deathly universe
with only a lonely love to whisper its feeble rebuke.

death:
i rise up against you
with these poems!

vengeful
as holocaust!

Poem For Lorca — Robert Lundquist

I heard someone say, I see, you are too lonely, too sad;
I see the mounds of sand, the tufts of earth watered by
your tears your friends suffering there beside you. No one
wants to hear this. Everyone wants to pretend this life at
this age is not this bad and then your cell phone rings and
the message left for you by a friend is asking you to un-
derstand, the thought of abandoning you is just a thought
and you begin to wonder, you think about the possibili-
ties left for you and the most probable is a form of can-
cer inherited from your mother. But consider this also,
consider the stars for one night, recognize them not as
your future but as the beams of light guiding you and your
children. The beams of light no one thought possible and
yet, here, lying in the cool grass you do understand the
planets more as your home, and you, no longer, insignif-
icant. Still, you know it is all coming off at the wheels, all
of it, because of the heat, even the tiniest of hairs and the
rough skin beneath, puff!—Paltry definitions of endings
when everyone is writing about beginnings and why not?
Waking up in the middle of the night scared shitless by
the same pain staying the same pain and not moving on as
pains that do not matter do. I am with, and for this pain.
I have no choice. But, I am also with and for the planets
that did not mean to be here, rising out of the same dust
as the rest of us only on a much larger scale but without
the responsibility that rises with a single, and that is all it
took, a single, breath. So breathe. Breathe deeply. Take
the smallest hand you can find and walk as far as you can
together. Always.

We Are Blessed — Robert Lundquist

A crescent moon hangs over us in a night whose stars, fall-
ing,
land in the grass outside a window far from the street
busy with everything purchased tomorrow
                         Not only everything hard
but everything soft because somedays we are kind to our-
selves,
even kind to the skin hanging a little to the left of center
breathing as fish
breathe

                                       in water
rising above the shores on which we stand waiting for our
boats to return,
and if the boats are late, our destination vanishes,
leaving behind what can only be traced by our children
who think they know us but the marks that truly define us,
hidden to ourselves
          in the end,
paper birds sleep on a ceiling keeping everything quiet,
                            everything quiet
hanging in an air of uncertainty
                    After all, we came here on our own,
                                no one
knew we were coming and if they did they would bring out
the sharp
objects
with terms upon which we could stay
                        Instead,
we keep our thoughts to ourselves,
standing steady in the dust coating our feet,
honored to be here.

Grenfell Rising — Lisa Luxx

Across the beauty salon
Where I get my eyebrows done
They speak of Grenfell Towers

In the pizza bar
Where musicians meet from near and far
They speak of Grenfell Towers

Through windows in the car I drive
Paused at traffic lights
I hear speak of Grenfell Towers

At the Aldi kiosk in town
Strangers less strange now
Speak of Grenfell Towers

They speak in Punjabi, in Patois, in Scottish
They speak in headlines, in hopelessness, in riot
We are engulfed in our own compassion
Suffocating in hate.

The lady with the hair dye
Drying high atop her head
Says 'we all know it could have been our families'
Then goes home to her sister's
Who, for tonight, will cook dinner
For all their loved ones,
Tomorrow they'll go to mosque
'And the door will be open if you'd like to join?'

The young girl in the waiting room says
'When you have nothing,
And you lose everything
It counts for so much more

Than if you'd had plenty
Before the fall.'

The pensioner in the tower block
Says she has not slept in a week
For her pigeon hole
On floor 23
Is in a building
That looks just like the one she watches turn to hell on TV
How can she sleep knowing her home is unsafe?
How can she sleep when the images she faces
In the news, are pictures she can place herself into?
How can she sleep when she knows
Night is when it comes for you?

The fire will not go out
It spat debris
So far
It landed in the hearts
Of everyone across this nation,
We are all burning inside now

Becoming a great 'we'.
Watching immigrants
Suffocate on smartphone screens,
Bound together by the story
Of those who stumbled through the dark
Over the trip hazard of their grandfathers
Into darker territory,
Yelling
'The smoke has come for me.'

Mohammad Alhajali
(Allah yerhamo)
Came for safety.
Whence most refugees drown in the sea
Our man was 14 floors high in flames;

In what world is that what refuge looks like?
His brother waited on the floor below
The echo of that empty space behind him
Will never go quiet again.
Survivor's guilt is a life imprisonment.

The wind carries the chorus of final words:
'I won't make it into work'
'Grazie, madre, per tutto quello che hai fatto per me'
'Tell my sons I love them'
'Ana aasef, ma'el salamah'

The fire will not go out.
The arms of our grief
Will never stop reaching again
Like flames chasing smoke
Into thin air above the eye-line
Of us; the littered shrapnel of despair.

And, you.
You, who plays the absent parent
While community comes together in siblinghood
Because they must.
You.
You who talks of terror attacks
Did you count the death toll
That you created on your own doorstep?
You.
You who heard screams for help
And sped off in a Benz
To make it clearer who meant less.

Your bunkers of safety
Are made from pound coins,
Coat of arms, dollar signs
Behind which you can hide
If you can stack them high enough.

Your barricade is our bodies
Your buried holes have irons doors
But I bet all the quid's we never had
That you ain't leaving us outside, under siege, anymore.

Across the windows of a council office
Comes the splat of a thousand paired palms!
The boot of a ladies foot!
As voices roar so loud
They become a foghorn
In the dark!
Whatever words they say
It means
'We are here, now
And we won't go away.'

Our ship has moored up
And the sound
Of our battalion's foot-steps
Chant 'we have had e-nough'.
Awake and riled up
Released from our cage
Because you made it that way.

The words justice and shame
Are plastered on the placards
That we need not hold,
This is not a demonstration
This is the real thing.
This is a battle cry.
This is what's been waiting in the wings.
We hold nothing here
But history
And we need our hands free
To push past your undeserving police.

You are not our government anymore

We dissolve you!
You are not our government anymore
We dissolve you!
You are not our government anymore
We dissolve you!
You are not our government anymore
We dissolve you!
You are not our government anymore
We dissolve you!
You are not our government anymore
We dissolve you!
You are not our government anymore
We dissolve you!

For those who never hit the ground
Who continue to fly through that endless night
Our heads crane to the sky
Forever waiting for you to arrive
Back into our arms.

So, across this nation we
Stretch. Holding hands.
Making the net you never had
So whenever you are ready
You may land
Safely, now.

Fuck 'Em - Damian Madden

Fuck the dream crushers and the nay-sayers,
Those inward looking perpetual frowners.
Fuck the can't lovers and pity-seekers,
Those poppy cutting bring you downers.
Fuck 'em.

Unflooded - Eleanor Malbon

it's not going to look like a city flooded
not here in this sheep paddock town
it's not going to be cyclonic winds of rain, hail
and afterwards muddied feet and tarp housing
here, it will be bushfires
burning forty metres high
heat-warped emergencies that you don't hear about
until the smoke obscures the sky
and the daylight is to hot to step into
it's not going to be pretty
but sometimes it will be pretty
the sun will still shine through
grass seeds in the evening
the moonlight will still turn
soft possum heads at night
a blue wren may hop through
anonymous bushes in the morning
some people will still see the people that they love
a couple might hold a wedding
with their feet between rubble and broken glass
halted cranes in the background
black against an ember-setting sky
maybe the tears in the eyes of a young woman
will warp the sight of the flames
so it seems like the Aurora Australis are
exploding in front of her in all their peaceful, touristic
glory
those warped flames in all their terrifying beauty

Invisible War Memorial - Anika Valentina Maric

In the forest where they lay down and wept
From secrets within their bones that were kept
Flowers sprung forth that were not of youth
Yielding to the mother of nature's truth

Eyes un-shielded to the glare of many suns
There are more wars won without any guns
Their hands cut through from scrambled trying
More battles lost, worse, with victims not dying

A heart is a stone that turns to gold dripping
Through cracks and chasms in-between slipping
Watching ships of love leave harbour forever
Unknown protection remains missions endeavor

Without a cup to collect drops of attention
Mouths gasp for hydrating words of connection
Morsels rot upon the leaves that they flourish
Mouths without bodies, whose souls they nourish

Electric Rent - Anika Valentina Maric

Shoot you dead, electronic head
I feel dead, so dead
From what you poured in my brain
Suddenly we all look the same
Don't you see what we've become
Our whole worlds come undone
No more understanding, sense or shame
Love and existence has become a game
Walking down this same grey road
Can't cope sensory overload
When you feel you need a friend
Click friend request and send
Now it doesn't even matter who
Fill emptiness with something to do
It's so boring waiting for the end
Choose another filter, play pretend
Don't you know it's a third world war?
But to you realities such a bore
So obsessed with how we look
Didn't notice what you took
Stole away our hearts and desire
Poured cold coca cola on our fire
But I'm a different kind of guy
It's so clear all you do is a lie
Melting this world down for scrap
Taking skin of our children's backs
 But I won't give my life up for rent
Going to live what's mine till its spent

Free as a... - James Massiah

Free as a mother-fucker
That's what I done
One time
One wild time
"Night night little one!
You could sibling my son
If one slips through!"
True? True!
Then how free is me
With that responsibility?
Free as I wanna be
That's how free, you no see?

Melting Pot — Chris McCabe

The United in Unites States
Has been described as a melting pot
In which anyone can contribute
To add to its coherence -
The pot simmers on a George Foreman grill.

The Poles stripped off & dipped
The Italians put on their Speedos
The Greeks waved from their Orthodox Church
And the pot melted into a single brew
Called English.

You want a job? Speak it.

Tenchdog — Chris McCabe

Tenchdog.
Trenchface.
The apple wormed in your mist.
Toadsnatch.
Turfwretch.
Snatcher in the tufted vetch.
Toewart.
Tankstart.
Transcendent of Grendel
made live for terrestrial.
Trump. Triumphalah! Twat.

The Artist - Devin Taylor McCarthy

She molded my lungs.
She wrapped herself around my face.
She seeped into my pours.

She meticulously took off my clothing.
Placed them on the ground.
And left me stark in front of the moon.
She stood back as the night sky drank me in and looked at me
as if I was her masterpiece.

THE TOWER OF BABYLON – Niall McDevitt

THE TOWER OF BABYLON IS A BLACK WICKER BASKET

SMOKING INTO THE AZURE OF PAST-PRESENT-FUTURE

WHERE THE UNACCOUNTABLE DEAD NO LONGER SPEAK

A THOUSAND LANGUAGES IN A THOUSAND WINDOWS.

*

THE CONFUSION WAS ONLY EVER BETWEEN TWO LANGUAGES:

THE LANGUAGE OF THE RICH / THE LANGUAGE OF THE POOR.

RICH MOUTHS, POOR EARS, THEY'RE LIKE CHALK AND CHEESE

POOR MOUTHS, RICH EARS, THEY'RE LIKE CHALK AND CHEESE

*

'WE WILL CLAD YOUR TOWER IN SUCH A DRESS OF BEAUTY

IT WILL STAND ON THE HORIZON LIKE A CATWALK MODEL'

AND LO! THE UGLY ZIGGURAT THEY BRANDED AN EYESORE

WAS NO LONGER ANATHEMA TO THE HIGH ONES OF BABYLON

*

'THANK YOU FOR PRETTIFYING OUR OUT-OF-DATE ZIGGURAT

BUT NOW WE DON'T FEEL 100% SAFE IN OUR OWN HOMES'

AND LO! THE RICH EARS ONLY LISTENED TO RICH MOUTHS

WHILE THE POOR MOUTHS CONTINUED WITH THEIR BABBLE

*

THE FLAMES OF THE GODS BURNT OFF THE DESIGNER GOWN

AND SPOKE A LANGUAGE NO ONE THERE HAD EVER HEARD

OF HELLS ON EARTH (OF HELLS ON EARTH)   NAKED

AND WALLS OF FUME (AND WALLS OF FUME)   BARE-FORKED

*

THE HIGH ONES OF BABYLON RESPOND IN RICH LANGUAGE

BUT NOTHING BUT NOTHING BUT NOTHING IS DONE

POOR MOUTHS WILL TELL THE 24 STOREYS FOREVER

BUT RICH EARS HAVE ALREADY MOVED ON (MOVED OFF)

She Was Here - Tabitha McKinney

Wrapped in cellophane like a book for sale. It is nuanced,
it is small and harrowing in the end.
Gum chewing, side-eying cigarette smoke
Siphoning its way through the crack of the car window.

Reformed-tweaker rants proselytized on steps / She was
here Every move. It is a night war laced with evidence.
Clueless.
Even unfeeling but not altogether numb.

Red lights turn corners, all bets off. The stage is set / one
last run
Just for the sake of a witness
To the siren.

Broken Spoons - Tenishia McSweeney

The dinner party fell away at the table,
With babies, broken spoons and dirty dishes still present,
all balancing on a stool.

There's nothing much to see now,
Except the echoes of that moment once flung up in the
air, and perhaps the lingering scent of excellence.

A reverberating noise rolled in, then washed out again as
fast, dragging those gurgling rocks with it, but we remem-
bered.
Waiting here for the full ache to set in
Or something.

Were we truly ready?

We no longer speak, for it has happened now.

Winter Lulls - Tenishia McSweeney

I lost all concept of time as the winter of your life set in
Running away through the hole of the world, attempting
to let it consume me in some other space that wasn't real.
To feel yet not feel as the pain set in tearing me apart in
slyness.

Howl – Amy Lou Miller

There's a delicacy to these strong winds that no
one seems to notice.
It sort of floats there in the eye of the storm,
converging yet observing.
It draws energy from the chaos around it, but is
leery not to draw attention.
I know this because I do the same thing. And I
find a vulgar thrill in it,
Because it is the only part of the storm
That remains

                    In the end.

Mojave – Amy Lou Miller

I come here not to sanctify its beauty or habit.
But for the very spectacle of warfare and tragedy
- For how can such thoughtful, inspired growth
Be doomed to a life of mere idleness?
Faint, pastel colors bob across the vast, flawless
sky,
Sugarcoating the knots and bends of the living
That are grotesque against the predictable tautness
of this desert ground. A crazed member of an
otherwise rapt audience;
Unforgiving, yet uncaring in its own right.
Even-tempered juniper and primrose stoke the
eye, But this wasteland looks well to the ways of
evil, Where fury is born of fault.
Every cordillera and dusty crag of this place reeks
of connivance. Of torture so ripe, only those
who've lived it can trace it.
These mountains are not in the least bit curious
about me, As the only ones they know are God
and The Devil himself.

Hammersmith Poem – Robert Montgomery

MODERNISM ISN'T A STYLE|
MODERNISM IS A DREAM
OF FREE EDUCATION AND
RACIAL EQUALITY AND
LIBRARIES FULL OF BOOKS
AND DREAMS NO LONGER
FULL OF TEARS/
THE AIR CHASES + SCATTERS
BLUE LIGHT MORE THAN IT
SCATTERS RED LIGHT>>
THAT'S WHY THE SKY IS BLUE
WHEN WE ARE CLOUDLESS
\WHEN IT IS BIG-GUSHED

AND THE SCREENS THAT
CIRCLE YOU LIKE BUTTERFLIES
NOW // ALL YOUR TOMOR-
ROWS TURNED TO ELECTRIC
WATERFALLS. MODERNISM
ISN'T A STYLE MODERNISM IS
A DREAM OF FAIR TAXATION
AND GENDER EQUALITY, A
RISE OF BEAUTY AND KIND-
NESS | A BLIND DREAM OF
LOVE, A PROMISE
OF CIVILISATION

MODERNISM ISN'T
ARCHITECTURE MODERNISM
IS AN ANTI-ARCHITECTURE, IT
IS THE REMOVAL OF WALLS
AND BORDERS| AND ONE
DAY WE WILL NOT GET SO
QUICKLY BORED OF MAGIC>
SPANISH GUITAR MUSIC ON
\THE BANKS OF THE THAMES
AND OUR CHILDREN FREE TO
WANDER EACH OTHER'S
CITIES AND MAKE NEW
UNIVERSITIES IN
THE STREETS

MODERNISM IS A PSYCHIC
LOVE WAVE | A BIG GUSH
OF SKY BREATH \
A SHIMMER OF KINDNESS
SUNG BY THE ANCIENT
EARTH / IT IS IN THE SILVER
VOICES OF THE WIND IN THE
TREES/ IT IS WILD AND HIGH
IN THE BEAUTY OF THE
WIND TURBINES THAT WILL
ONE DAY SCYTHE THE HAIR
OF THE TROGLODYTE
TRUMP

Song to the Sleeper - Lilli Moors

Close your eyes
and the room will leave you

See the black void of air that breathes you

For you it was born
and for you it will fade away like your eyes

wide white
rolled back
in the hole of your head that the birds have left for heat
and deserts

And the wounds will be scars and the scars will be
pale
white marble

skin

This house of yours the lights are on but no one's home

Fragments of thoughts like insects
crawling in white spit of indifference

Inside you
a jungle
a blood hungry explosion of bliss and emptiness

Bang bang
I wish I had a heart since there a craters of shattered glass
in cold screen skin

I wish I was you king-size shadow
at the bottom of things of thoughts
of void
loud aortas systems of nerves veins blood
Silently streaming consciousnesses selling dreams
Open your eyes
Vacuums of lust and vacuums of sleep

Abdi's Blue Guitar - Nick Moss

Abdi has a blue guitar
It's plastic, has broken strings,
Found it in a skip.
He carries it for protection,
Pitches and reels
Along Harlesden High Street,
Picking up fag ends
While carrying his blue guitar

In Mogadishu TFG military
Rammed a rifle up his arse.
In a West End shop doorway
Someone poured petrol
Set his legs on fire.
He staggers now
Can of brew in one hand
Spilling, still carrying his blue guitar.

All time to come just torment
No rhapsody, no screeching jay
No Dichtung, just pain
Lurching, shitting blood
"The discord merely magnifies."
Abdi has a blue guitar
No one ever asks
To hear him play.

The Carpenter — Sophie Naufal-Baker

I am a carpenter.
I carve the future from the past,
Alas
I cannot make the present gasp.
I cannot make it mould and swell.
Not well.
On rotten wood I dwell.

I am a welder.
That nestles in old iron fists
And they like ancient cysts
That, though I try, I can't resist

I am a fishmonger.
That fixates on the blood she spills
And writhing 'tween those scales and gills,
For thrills,
Without the will and seldom still

I am a carpenter.
I carve the future from the past,
And make the buried curl and gasp

If only I could hold a match up to a woody tentacle.
If only I could see it catch enlightened flames and tumble.

Sunfish - Elizabeth O'Connor

Note: in September 2016, a group of scientists recording
fish off the coast of Perth found that several species 'sang'
at the arrival of dawn, as birds do. They attempted to find
similar patterns elsewhere, but were unsuccessful.
In the tired roots of the
seabed, the light is sent
to gather us. The water is a snake
charmed out of its skin, warm-blooded
and boneless. Beneath the airborne world,
our language is one of weight; the unimagined
lightness of swimming,
the heaviness of a drowned forest.
Ours are birds of rock and sand,
a chorus of black and green;
the whistle of air between
pine needle teeth
silvers the spines of our bodies;
immutable and hidden, stretching
over us like a fallen moon.
When the dirt glitters, it speaks
of a different world;
the orange light is a gift.
How it arrives like breath,
how it makes the
weeds glow
like flames.

Waiting til Spring - Elizabeth O'Connor

Crystal's cup is clear
and steaming, hot water
coddled by her hands. Three
days of snow and Shanghai
is far, its roads gravelled
thick with salt, she tells me;
her parents told her.
The river behind her flats has frozen,
comes split with an orange cat;
a fat one, she tells me,
round and lost.

A Precarious Existence - Hande Oynar

When I woke up today
I wanted to die a little
For no apparent reason
Other than to see the sweet fish of life
Jump again
In my belly
The iridescent little fish
That tells me I have something in me
Waiting to come out
Or making me imagine things
Like the old lady who lives in a raggedy apartment filled
with broken antiques from a glamorous era
Who told me "there is nothing to be ashamed in life.
Nothing."
Like the panther that I met on a wooden tower where I was
having tea with my lover
And casually walking down the creaking stairs
He stealthily following me
I stealthily smelling his patterns
Only to realize
I am alive.

Lazy Sunday - Kayleigh Parle

Trying to love my body feels impossible
Trying to accept it is the nearest goal I can hold on to.
I'm so angry at it.
At how much time its taken up of every day since I was a
teenager
Time that my male counterparts had the luxury of think-
ing in.
I break down every time that I try to push forward
It's so exhausting that I just end up trying to ignore it
But I love you. And I want to love you.
You're closing in on baring your soul
So days are darkening and I'm losing my mind!
I need more time. But what good would that do me?
I've had two years too long of having you in my heart and
in my head
but not in my hands. Hardly in my space.
I love you and I need to find some way to stretch over
these walls walled around me
So that when you reach out to me, I can reach back.
You are all thats in my heart, and these days
I could really use a lazy sunday with you
After all this pain, we deserve each other
But my dark passenger takes up all of the bed
So clothes are left on. Scenarios shut down before they're
created.
Outside, the moon dominates the sky like a torchlight
Demanding answers. Who's looking for me tonight?
I know you're out there, looking for the words.
I'm looking for the truth, for the receptor
To be able to do something with those words
When my beloved delivers them to me.
I can't be here bleeding lonely anymore
At the mercy of a sickness stuck stubbornly in my life.

Armour - Verity Pemberton

The house could not contain their sadness,
 a shadow of thoughts followed their every step.
Heavy like stone it dragged at the threads of their being,
snake skin crisp and hollow it pulled and took something
away that could never be replaced.

Dull tones.
Lead heavy lids and salted skin,
So kind, so kind.
The words were just letters.
They didn't help.

I - Eleanor Perry-Smith

And on days we don't remember
At times we can't believe
lost you 'cross the water thrashing in our tumbled weeds

Timber! Call to savior
Bombs away! We sing
Frayed ropes send us adrift

Fighter pilot lenses
that's right, the pilot fights
Slides upon the surface
Women's faces
Bombs away.

I tried, I tried to tell you that the storm was riding high
and all we'd slopped together with wet mud and limestone
tries
Was nothing to the power
the hum and din
of Mind

Then I tried, I tried to tell you that all's a tiny lie
but screaming at the altar bubbled down with pride
shoes bloated, speaking tongues, naked feet astride

Never, Mind, not a thought
the wrong word and the hell it wrought
a joke the pilot tells, and laughs generations long

The New Normal - Margaret Perry

First, it was a pool of yellow water
gathering in the hall in the same shape
every day. Mornings she passes
the bloom of it, wonders about the number
of a plumber. The vigilante in No. 77
thinks it's piss. Yesterday she found him
lying in wait by the lifts.

Then, the lights started to flicker
the stairs by night glimmer and glitch.
Mornings she thinks, I should call someone,
an electrician. Evenings she feels
down the hall in the gathering dark,
too tired to care. After all,
it's a communal area.

First, she thinks she can't bear it
this ache gathering behind her eyes
but as months go by, they adjust.
She grows so accustomed
to the voltage disruption
that she stops noticing.

I am glad I am not made of glass — Margaret Perry

He dresses gingerly,
jeans and a t-shirt with long sleeves
to hide the gleam of the sun on the shards
of his spiky elbows. Covers his head.
Steps out. Nowhere special to go.

In a sea of suits she hurries through the City
and thinks when did I and then stops thinking

A hand outstretched on the pavement ahead
he empties his pockets and is suddenly
completely light. Later at the pub, he says
do you take card, I haven't got any

MORNING EVERYONE
Before coffee she sends half a million pounds
into the ether she used to be nervous when she
but it's just loose change round here

Later at the pub people laugh at his jokes and he
longs to be elsewhere he thinks when did I
stop letting myself be alone?

She has been round here three years.
Can you believe it's been three years
over a gingernut biscuit at break
someone else makes tea so she
feels bound to at least make
some conversation.

Later still in bed he is alone at last
the coldness of it like a gasp
in the dark he reaches for his iPhone
and scrolls, and scrolls, and scrolls.

She wakes up
She wakes up
She wakes up
She wakes up
She wakes up
She wakes up

and another week peels away. Thank God for the person
who made the calendar, she thinks on her commute
other times she thinks she has been duped by the weeks
sneaking on so smoothly one after another like someone
has planned them. She blurts to the man in the hat sat
at he right hand — who decided today was a Tuesday in
June?
Pope Gregory the Eight, he says, without missing a beat.
She checks her watch and does not notice the light, pris-
med
at the tip of the man's index as he dings for his stop.

He pulls his hat down over his silica ears
as he steps off the rail replacement bus.
Crowds are tricky and he walks slowly
eyes peeled for trip hazards like buggies or dogs
or people on phones — he holds tight to himself
and dreams he is nothing but sunlight covered in skin.

She reminds herself to be grateful for the little things.
The gathering of the days into a life she prayed for
when she used to pray. Head bent, hurrying now
her office glistens in her peripheral vision, punching
into the sky —

Smell of lilies. Huge windows guillotine the light
into oblong portals on the floor. His feet have brought
him
to the foyer of a City branch of an investment bank.

Can I help you?
He shakes his head. Steadies the rest of him.

Head bent, hurrying now, she's thinking of nothing,
nothing, when she bangs into a man with a hat in his
hands
bolting out the foyer door and he

    shatters   on   i m
p
          a
c
   t

Oh excuse me
she says uselessly to the shards splintering the concrete.
At reception she dials up for a cleaner to sweep up the
glass,
drop the clothes to a charity shop. Later at her desk,
hands battering keys, she feels a twinge —
a glimmer lodged in her palm, piece of rarefied sand,
swelling the flesh.

In the Rain — Barbara Polla

I was lying on him
Him naked so was I
And his sperm in a cloud
Was dropping upon us
Like the tears in the rain

I was lying on him
He was like a boat
Floating boat in the fog
His mouth in my neck
Whispers in the rain

I was lying on him
Swimming on his body
Exploring geography
And he was like the sun
Shining in the rain

I was lying on him
I was loving his skin
Listening to his body
Listening to his mind
Singing in the rain

I was lying on him
Him naked so was I
And his sperm in a cloud
Was dropping upon us
Like the tears in the rain

Our Doom Song - Mick Ray

I said I don't like prophecy
You said you like to know the ending first
I sighed and looked out the window
For a sign
But the sparrows were sharp
And good looking
Against the city's dull neon whites

I took too long
I know
in choosing the canned food
for the apocalypse
you've planned,
but my sins
are soft
and civilized

Tell me again
how these stars
form a pattern
of the hanged man
and how
I will soon be lost
and raving

I have uniforms and rations
the best perfumes
the three important books
I've written the new constitution
we'll start over from this new beginning
I will learn to build a house for you
and fight tigers hand to hand
if it comes to this

for now the sun is shining
and the air is still
and sweet

with orange blossoms
the sparrows have come for the sage
and lavender
but the rosemary is overgrown with spiders

Treaty of Serpents — Mick Ray

Take this venom
it will not heal you
or keep you young
but the taste
will be so unforgettable.

Walter Whitman your Americans
came out wrong
but we came so close in the soft night's light
the purr of your cat
on your shoulder
in your father's pencil factory

your hands paper cut
and small in the darkness
disintegration always your favorite effect
as you enter the room
in a cloud of smoke

teacups chipping
the bells are ringing
charming men have risen
speaking softly to your whisper
but only I can see the assassin
waiting on your lips

the snakes have arisen
and you have laid them in your bed
tomorrow
we will talk more about religion

A Chorus Sounds - Edd Ravn

Waving them goodbye with his eyes
Focusing on everyone meant no one
They sent farewells into the air with hands and sounds
Feet on the shore
There were naked children swimming and playing

Water ran over the ink and the ink was unable to remain
single and still
Running to create moments and movements
Not marks or streaks
The surface a pool of present

Is repetition the meaning or the feeling
Am I repeating myself in a different language
Do you know who this portrait looks like

At the back of the boat a physics teacher
Jumps away into the water waving
Goodbye to his cap and ten merry school boys
Running the rope attached to the boat through his hands
until
He was a good forty foot away but
A jerk and the distance still increasing meant
He hadn't been able to hold on

The sails open
The sails full
A sense of excitement

Is repetition the meaning or the feeling
Am I repeating myself in a different language
Away from people and onward towards the quiet.

Sebastian — Jeremy Reed

Self-appointed saint of depravity
on Meard Street's vampish wet-feet odour,
reluctant millennial survivor
of Soho's sanitised clean-up
creeped walk-ups - your maverick diatribes
sensationalised dinner parties,
eating your own hand like a cannibal
in a black frock coat and red sequinned vest,
we's meet at Home House, you the opener,
me the featured glamour poet,
you so coked it was like astral travel,
and under it the abashed alienation
of intimidated bravura,
the ordinary tack of being Sebastian,
the kindness you gave to the vulnerable,
the terrible fear of the impostor
being denuded as fake, the shyness
layered with affect - it don't come easy
living that way at the point of a gun
kept under the pillow - never forget
a burnt-orange light mellowed on Meard Street,
me passing through you sat on your doorstep,
and your soft-eyed estrangement seeing me,
having you rise, so tall it seemed hours,
embrace me wordlessly and sink back
into icy self-preoccupied distraction.

Doncha Bother Me — Jeremy Reed

Arrogant as leather
but it's introspective shy,
I'm diffidently unapproachable
except by losers on the street
rubbed out like black pips on a dice
by rain - do what I do you
get lonelier than the Shard's spike
in frozen scrolls of cloud,
it's like a large abstract pursuit
on a grey moon - identiless
word-trafficker, a laureate
of puddled squares, personable cafes,
cute pick-ups, can't go anywhere
without attention to my look's
fascinating ambiguity,
just write it down like the Chinese
a betting slip - that's poetry
no more no less - the odds reduced
I'll ever get it right
clean on the chin. It's what I do
right to the ends of afternoons
toned mango and yellow in hazy grey
for no money or even least status
as anyone or anything
in what the world calls meaning, my own way
of facing into the red fading evening light.

Orphic Egg – Anna Rieser

coddled til bone dry
a sprat wriggles in
dwindling yolk
all unconscious unctuousness
turned dust.

rhemy whites
smoke through water
stream to rubber
without the shell.

Did it sheild or incase?
trap or protect?

prisoned the fertilised
who rise archaeopteryxian
to airyer lofts
or acts as brahmanda
to those who need
to a firmer set.

how to tell
soft boiled gold
from sickly chalk?
If only eggs could talk.

Basic Bitch - Anna Rieser

In their poor lit kitchen
I remember what I had forgot
How marble I was
Turning cold ear and smiles
To words that glance
And chip at
Composite world.

So small to think
Transversing veins
Were all the network we need.

Air thrums with it
Impenetrable and I am shy

Won't fall to coyness
Gape, carp and caper
Soft shell fragmented
Where I thought it might bend.

And I am all surface
Skin hungry and Marsyas
Poor tanned by small brain
So untouched opal-ed to black

Hubris to enter with a lowly pipe
Pipe squeak pipsqueak
Galleys gall cured
Bitter black bileb
For basic bitch

Cameo Pink and Slow Black - Rebecca Mary Roose

She is so ensconced in the soft pink,
All wrapped up and spread out neatly
In Cameo, in Amaranth, laced up
In the jewelled paleness of exquisite youth.
Fertility dancing and dispersing feverishly
Into shaped words and lengths of divine
All backed up by privilege and
Numbers on paper,
Spinning beneath arched gilded halls and
Falling into painted walls,
Decorated alcoves in bioluminescence.
Eyes and noses in oil paint watch over her.
Painted strokes witnessing her luck
Under chandeliered light,
Catching the scent of something sweet—
But it is all fleeting.
Those painted faces have watched other girls spin.
They have watched other gleaming girls
Laugh, dance, and clasp hands with tall lovers.
And here am I—
Draped in slow black, I am dark shade.
All rosewood like blood and rich Byzantium,
Depths you can fall into.
Typing out words with pianist's fingers,
Kissing lips and giving time—
Half to mobile screens, half to chasing
Piles of books and ivory cult dreams.
I am pierced with beseeching green orbs.
Serving coffee for numbers, and hating it.
Writing letters for recognition, and hoping.
And I am still getting to know my face, its shape,
My eyebrows, my limbs, my loins.
Still rising from mind-graves,
Pushing on divides and borderlines,

Watched by spiders from high ceilings in
A plush rental, a palace for seeking queens
And watched by the faces of friends
Printed on the walls in black and white,
Attempting history
But most likely to be forgotten.

LDN- Rebecca Mary Roose

I had the inky black, there.
It was there that I had dances
Beneath gunmetal clouds
Hiding stars and moonlight.

Spinning in gated parks and
Leaving liquor behind in plastic cups,
I had a little shimmer on my skirt
In shining goldenrod velvet.

It was short, and my legs were long
Possibilities that went on forever,
Slender porcelain skipping and buckled
Into shining black-booted glory.

The smell of Toni & Guy shampoo
And the clink of the butter dish in the kitchen
Didn't mean much then, but are
Irretrievable halleluiah's melting soft now.

The squirrels climbed stairways to heaven
On the trees outside my window every morning,
While I climbed into plush white
To lay down my sleepy head in dawn light,

Camberwell-grey and under the glint
Of sly fox eyes. At some point, you realise
The city is a globed expanse
Made up of more cloud and less sky.

That she keeps you holed in and bolted down,
Dancing dolls in a miniature dominion.
Crowning nature with obliterating stone structures,
Burnt umber town houses guarded by cats and

All the doorways you pass through and
Flee through and seek shelter under when it rains.
And like that you find yourself a gleeful ghost
Haunting the streets, the underground, the faces you pass.

You are captured, you are history, you are hers,
Your heart is beating a love unrequited.
For she, the goddess in grey, is all smoke and sex,
Husked chills and grime for tongues to fight over.

She is chemical plumes rising into blanketing clouds,
Snaking out into tracts and lungs and like that
We are all beckoned and trapped in silent bondage,
Our hearts blooming blackening roses.

Le Cirque des Femmes - Rebecca Mary Roose

Wild earth, wild earth,
I have lost all my girls.

Those sacred nights dressed up in black,
The way black is the holiest colour.

Wild earth, wild mother,
How funny it is—the dispersion.

How easy independence seems when
Relying on the light of un cirque de femmes!

To carry you higher and onwards and
Handing out laughs with

Curled hair twined around hair
And warm skin on skin

On golden skin
And brassy liquid dances.

See how light is all but a trick of the eye?
Voir comment toute la lumière est fugace!

And with this little cirque des femmes
Goes my sense of solidarity.

Wild mother, ferocious lover,
I am a lonely thing.

I am brandishing retentions,
I am learning to cling

And missing my blazing fire on strings—
That surreptitious puppet-wonder.

Girls are demons.
They pull you under.

No Title - Onur Safak

We heard some stories
She's doing porn

Web camera performances
She said

There's a sense of mutual respect between her and I
I know where she is living

You want me to go with you
Might be you know her

We walked to her house on the other side of Notting Hill
She grew chrysanthemums by the door
Inside is a mess of art supplies

We are just here for a talk
She started to share her entire life offline with us
But I avoid to talk
And write poems on my phone in the corner

Luz - Sebastian Sanchez-Schilling

On an overcast afternoon,
diced by toothpick trees,
through the curtain's crack,
light still comes to me.

Nostalgia - Stefanie Schefter

it's something
just a little too sweet
something
maybe a little rotten
like a peach left out in the sun
its insides liquefying in the heat

it's like
pressing on a bruise, halfway down your shin
a dull familiar ache, deep under the surface
a tiny galaxy of dead cells and old blood—
the aftermath of the collision.

it's passing your younger self on the street
and turning just a minute too late, missing her forever

it's sliding backwards into memories
and spending whole days with ghosts
in empty rooms, inside a house that isn't yours anymore.

but it's all so familiar, you'll say. it feels just like before
—that slant of the light, the smell of cinnamon, the way it
feels to laugh, right here

did you know that the word 'nostalgia' means 'to return
home'?
it also means 'pain'

how's that for poetry?

Farewell - Oliver Schick

Listen, hush now—did you hear the pinging of the bell?
 As you walk back to that corner in your earnest thoughts,
Follow your mind's eye, you tingle with a haunting spell.
It is just as clear as ever, one no time distorts.

There you see a secret ghost with windows brightly lit.
It does not appear to everyone, just those who know
That it pierces any veil that they put over it.
If you cherish what's been here, you'll find its homely
glow.

Sometimes, it is muted, as if electricity had gone.
Then there are two candles on each table, mild of light,
And the windows look like satin laid upon the night,
And the sprites inside are packed in tight and pale and
wan.

There they listen to old music in new greens of spring,
Songs within their melodies and other songs without,
And new music in old dresses it's abandoning,
And you strain to hear more clearly, but you're racked by
doubt

That it ever really happened, that it's not a trick.
It's too good to ever have been true, you say again,
But the sprites brush past your heart that's like a kindling
wick,
And you burn once more like you were burning way back
then.

Built from bricks made from a vanished field of fertile
days,
That old place will stir you for all time and won't be still.
Everything must go—but that which is undying stays.

It's forever tethered to the fondness of your will.

Then you see that one of these transparent sprites is you,
As you used to be and as you never could foretell.
You can feel their quiet whispers through and through.
Can you hear the pinging of the bell? It says farewell ...

Flatus Voci – Jennifer Francesca Sciuchetti

I watched tighten the wrists.
First,
    the one.
Then,
    the other.
Nervous, they said to me.

With the oblique look
I watched your fingers brandish the nails
Forcing them to curl along a vertical axis
Whose loose tongue declined poetry.

I perceived
In the stiff angle of your lips
A whisper of pain
Stifled by the uncertainty
Of words never pronounced.

Dim and indelible light
Crouched on the interrupted surface
Of your intimate fears
Pregnant in the act
Of assimilating grotesque newcomers.

The Magnificent Sunset of Thrills - Ana Seferovic

first you would hear the
metal garden gates
a loud bang
and then her high-heels
smashing the concrete
with the power of a CEO
causing a tight mixture
of anticipation, anxiety and
a weird feeling of guilt

for no obvious reason-

mummy is home

with suitcases full of
sweets for children
and nicely packed
stories for grown ups

mothers
oh those mothers
oh mothers mothers

tough blondes in charge
of surface mining
of men digging
/he is alive, he is well,
he is inside
earning, producing/

mothers not interested
in children
producing children
producing clean sheet,

serving food

serving entertainment

there was no entertainment
no
no entertainment

once she was offered a
house in a holy land
she refused it
she didn't want to live there
she said it was too flat and
there was no birds

flat pancake of the holy land

no not for me sir

she also said that in some
countries, where she was
on her business trips
there was no cotton pants

you had to wait for your
 turn to buy them

with your bare bottom?
children would ask chuckling

and that in another place
women had the longest legs
she had ever seen
and they were drinking
for a medial
smashing their long bony knees
on old cobbled streets

she tried eels
and frogs
 and snakes and jelly
like desserts
drank martinis
and black russians
and white russians

and fly airplanes

where lunches were nicely
packed in a plastic tray

(she would always bring little
satchels of sugar and salt
and plastic cutlery with the
logo of the airline home)

and that in some places she
was followed by an agent
who would tell her if she

had gone too far

you always have to go too far
to understand
the cold drinks
from
the cold war
brown drink cabinets

we all went too far

that morning on her 37th
birthday she looked at
herself in the mirror
and finally understood

that weird expression
on her mother's face
she noticed as a child:

I observed her from her window;
she was thin
always looking like a
girl from a faraway
good bone structure
people would say

now in her memory, it
was always sunset
roofs tops and tree tops
sinking slowly into the
sticky apricot sunset jam
everything was just
floating there

and her mother
floating there too

weightless

smoking

smoking like those cowboys on
horses riding off into the horizon
smoking like those french stars
in their convertibles, curving
above the mediterranean
smoking like a free woman
lingering in a bar, ready
for some new loving
like a secret agent

like bond, james bond

that was how she looked to her
puffing those hours
and hours away
floating in warm sunsets
but her weird expression
was always a mystery
until that morning, when she
saw her own face in the mirror:
swollen eyes, endless boredom.

yes, that's it!

her mother was bored.
and that was a special kind
of elaborate boredom
boredom of a factory
worker who decided he would
stay forever in a factory
he didn't like
who decided that every
day would be the same and
not quite satisfactory
but that every day
would be familiar
and that was good enough
not the boredom one feels
when there is nothing to do
this was boredom where
everything was boring
the very essence of her
universe was boring
this apricot sunset
just materialised
reassuring boredom

she understood her

mother's face now
and she loved her
more than ever

around the place where
she was smoking
a circle of cigarette buds
was spreading like
an upside down halo
like a little stage
waiting for her to come back
and conduct yet another
magnificent sunset of thrills

The Postcard - Ana Seferovic

Lately we are going to the woods very often

Woods are for grownups

Early mornings as well

When we are not sleeping
When we are not dreaming –
 of ships

For grownups is closeness
For grownups are lenses
Microscopes and washing machines

Laying around the streets
Used up knees
Rolled up in a blanket like a burrito
Freedom is corpulent
Freedom is calorific
Has greasy palms
Cracked heels

The carpet at the main square is soaking up
The hunger

Beyond the curtains
Cats are wriggling
Cockerels are disturbing

Princess's Earrings are growing
Night and Day is growing

Quiet brutality is breathing
Common as nose bleeding

Boys are growing

Boys and fists

At the end of the day
She envies you for
Ocean freshness of monumental
Vertigo high concrete-queens

That are entering through your window

Through which legs, newcomers are arriving
Big eyes
Big
Appetite

At the end of the day
She envies you on loneliness
She envies you on
Farawayness

The Reversed Heart - Ana Seferovic

She can see the faraway ships
But not as far away as she is

She can see the clouds
Very shallow
And not so reversed as her

Reversed heart is

And very clearly she can notice that the
Surface is only the surface

Velvety and effortless

Beautiful

Easily disturbed- as sand

You will be fine little girl
As long as you glide

And glide

Just like a geometrical point:

Without dimensions
But with the perfectly determined position

The Unicorns of Punjab - Afshan Shafi

This morning is full of Unicorn.
I am as certain of them
as the claw-footed serenader
east of the summer mosque

The gutters lie bellyful with
chromatic waters; Unicorn scruff.
Impression recorded by a street peddler :
a blue and pink beast
a fettle of oxygen

Unicorn you are so early and detergent brash.
You efface the cottony sunrise
to thinnest wound.
Your one accomplice; a chestnut foal
whose bashful parley
wettens the farthest steeple
Oh Unicorn do not pretend I live for your white lashes
portending regicide,
over our muddy cantonments

I feel your mother must be a saint
and you drawn out of a glassy womb
to sheer plastic placenta
How the heliotropes glistened at the moment
of your bodily confession
How the ailing tigers stood listening to your scarlet music
in their pens.

Unicorn your three days in Punjab were kismet;
orange groves were draped in Keffiyeh's
while grasshoppers tickled your hooves to
ecru.
You are so famished and private
like an excellent study in oil
If they vacuumed all the nothing choux of the
sky

they would find your face medallion there
your presidential likeness.
Oh Unicorn there are too many of you now
from Latvia and Beijing
they descend on helicopters and sky-junk
landing on earth with a springy giggle,
stomachs full of pins.

Miss A. and Dog - Afshan Shafi

We began life you and I
as a child exorcist and her consort
you wore such a spectacular necklace of pebbles
and I an apron of electrodes
Our family left us in the museum for days
where we wrote operas for the statues
our poor melodies ringing out
against the whistling chasm
there was no one to see us   to see us being brave
only the music of the fall
for you and I
beating with green thunder.
barren to a fault and judicious
we hung our heads amongst the prim da Vinci's
fasted amongst the ceramic oceans
the bleeding crustaceans.
It is you and I dog till the edge of the steaming forests
they are rolling the land from under our feet the
bog-thick rugs
the bird-rich winter
Dog rake this chill heat
or hold it for a second against your bones
fawn architect.
Answer me a few, to impede solitude.

Where does dog thrive?

amongst the mulberry thorns. in a gold pagoda covered
with white truffles. beneath the rain in its slipshod veer.
beneath a troop of ragdolls, a fluency of grosgrain. nest-
ing amongst the sparrows and here they freed my soul in
preservative. prattling amongst the slick nuns. their tiaras
of dead bees.

Dog what did it feel like in the birthing pools?

dry heat. sub-aquatic jackal. I scurried in the dust. a

bludgeoned critter. belly up I counted each of my legs.
they were eels moving under a blinding sea roof.
The climate was tuned by clouds in the shape of gravid
women. I was the world's gushing infant.

Who gave you your name?

No one. I carried my title in my left paw like a stanchion.
It still hurts. a fine pink charge disturbs the center from
time to time. this is when glass starts peeling off walls
How will you correct death?
by seeking it. nuzzling its hash panniers. spending time
with it in its bombed out boudoir. All those bavarian
looking-glasses.

How will you arrive at courage?

by falling off. into oceans led in successive tremolo.
flutter-tongued. by falling off suburban roofs where the
skies are italicized purple. by looking for old languages at
the roof of my mouth. Remember when the sabre-shark
ripped through the gloss of the museum? It left its left eye
and a rustling fin. for days emitting an urgency beyond
the circumstancial. courage is like that. an eye suspended
for days in the fray. a crochety poltergeist.

How will you correct the forgotten?

by tearing their plaid smocks. gnashing their crusty plastic
trinkets. biting those pustuled love-warblers. where love
is unrequited Dog cannot flow through. though Dog is
the only one who can cure the forgotten of their transpar-
ency.

Dog what is blindness like?

God's dark pram. He tossed me past the seedy cobbles of
Dublin. Not without bruises. Pulmonary lucidity. Pyro
running over rivers. Gin-geologic. Imagine the mother
keel of five rivers. Before Dog spoke in his patois of ether.

before Dog was spoken of as a wretch. Drowned in quilts of smoking satin.

Dog, when will we meet again?

When the suns are black. And the waters yellow. I will come from between the vertical wave as it is deafended by sky.

I will bring your coals unspoken. pretty regrets.

I will always carry your sorrow within my heart of hearts.

That Street... - Ásta Sigurðardóttir

that street in neighbourhood filled wit
h dew
from lampposts 3 meters high
shallow puddle clear like apron plastic
from the corner store
one for making dinner love
lived above the bank/nectar pizza shop
more porncorners then gasstation and
sometimes both combined

yellow tooth phone offering a trip
loaded with presents we ate and then n
o t
another morning nothing

notesin white folded shee ts
glued the top with names in front

it went to air and back again never
and all in things we left behind

Half of the Whole - Amber Singh

If I give you my love,
take it.

Although
you'd be a fool to take it too personally.
You see I'm in love
with nearly half of the whole
of this wide winded existence.

I am hopeless-
an overbrimming hopestress
Because there are

too many
warped and weathered trees
casting shadows under the moon-

too many
pieces of trash in the gutter
that flood me with a sense of déjà vu-

too many
kindred eyes with buckled knees
found in the sideways light of the afternoon.

If I give you my love
Take it.
It's personal.

But if you hold out your hand for my heart's currency,
do not second-guess the exchange rate when you see the
same coin

in the pocket of a crooked tooth
or the death grip heat of June
or with a man 5 feet taller than you.

There is enough love to give.
We can always make more.

Brighton - Pollie Sortain

Brighton,
The night time uncovers your secrets, You turn into a
playground,
Your streets get louder,
People dance wherever there is music, Discos cover you
every night.

In summer and winter alike, People cover your beaches,
Girls scantily clad in December. From sunrise to sunset,

You are never alone.

There is something magical,
About watching the sunrise on the beach,
At 6am with greasy chips in one hand,
And a spliff in the other,
The calming sound of the tide kissing the pebbles.

The twenty-four-hour cafes,
Filled with twenty-something-year-olds, Enjoying greasy
food at 4am,
Before the stubble back to their beds to sleep, Until the
sun goes down,
And they come to play with you again.

Brighton,
You will never be alone.

You'll Burn For This - Scott Temple

Analeptic sin drifted in. We were dabbling in wet orifices.
Heathens damned to the sewers by generic onlookers.
Saccharine medicine blotting drenched pretences. We
could die in this forsaken mess. Black lace, leather boots.
Lots of hair. Nerves jacked enough to peel corridors for
crystal tears. The familiar odour of a burning dream. A
room of lies, of hungered cries and echoes of staunch
regret. Bruised flesh prisms. Woven limbs shimmer a
tapestry of perspiration spent. Gaping mouths await a lit-
tle death. The wallpaper burns cosmic acrylic blue. Skin
flowers. Kindling psyches lit with dark humour intention.
Up go the effigies to jazz and runaway dawns. Instru-
ments of lust wear grinning masks to the sacrifice. Dying
before the price of expensive taste. A nightly frequency of
love's abandon. Turn out lights in a city of love and march
the streets in solitude. The breeze presses the curtains
and sighs through the window. Drowning in hotel suite
dreams.

A Winter of Two I - Ramo Thek-Zeroual

We were not in love, we were sad
Through all those long evenings
We sat on the naked flour
And started winter and writing
You helped me to snatch the bones of loneliness from my
bones
And I helped you to sleep with a hand on your heart
To escape hearing agony

In a time when talking about wars is forbidden
But fighting for everything is a virtue
We entered the gates of tomorrow
Like beaten soldiers
We invented blue mothers
Who abandoned us every night
And when nothing was enough to justify our sadness
We said we were poets
And talked about losing and heartbreak

We were not sad, we were in love
Yet the silence had a reserved seat between us
Everywhere
You followed me without asking if a company is needed
I followed you without saying thank you
We used to share cigarettes and talk about heartbreak
In no language

Paris Burnings - Ramo Thek-Zeroual

Paris is still burning
Cigarettes and stock lists
Paris is still burning baguettes
Burned bread for a Syrian refugee
Dark and bitter like the taste of waiting in front of the im-
migration office
Paris is still burning
Under the heavy eyelashes of the night
Velvet touch is how I call my beret
Set fire to canals and to the diamond tear drops of the
Ritz
And make it a flamboyant dance floor where life is a
magazine in motion
The shelter seeker has crossed the lines of death
With a dream made of bread and wine
Let them eat the smoke of cigarettes and the smell of
freshly baked croissant
keep the city safe
Dance or die
Dance or die

Ghost - Ramo Thek-Zeroual

Alone you are
The memory of love is empty despite the crowd
Your cups are coffeeless
And the darkness of cacao smells like crying
A ghost sits on your table
Although you will never admit that it's yours
Under your feet there is a surprising emptiness
It saddens the sky
Here you are, trying to be a poet for the last time
With your same old empty desire of paper and pen.

Two poems - Sophie Thompson

I.
Waltzing on the rubble fancy-free debris
Diagnoses a saturnine child
A posy of perils
lily-pondering in corrosion
sharper than forget-me-nots
like how ring a ring a roses is about falling
My dosage increase dullness increase
If I were a colour I'd be beige
And the Northern Line, once lullaby now migraine
Junction damp dripping to chews now tarred beneath
shoes smog
This smog big smoke
Fumigating menthol
Take me to cottonwood buttercups neat chins
Glowing can you untangle my hair
Please, it can be such a weighty mess

2.
Be wary of boys with bookshelves weightier than their
brevity
warning sign of a wanderlust tasting tongue
I'm glad you're older than me but I wish I wasn't younger
than you.
It's like
sometimes I wish you lived closer and
sometimes I wish you food poisoning.
Tell me I sound like a song
(ink wrists and I'll become one)
Tell me you still like my face and then "I don't want
To be your goddamned Humbert"
Spreading like ivy across your skin and
pressed forget-me-not in dog-eared pages
Tell me I sound like a song
(but you'd written the song for a stranger with a shared

name)
But Sal Paradise wouldn't smoke an electronic cigarette
But you've only seen those freckles you so liked four times
But I don't want to be your skin, your soul
Not even your Dolores
Claiming you were a growing pain whilst I was nothing
more
Than a writing prompt

Sea Glass - Poppy Turner

hold it inside your pocket —
get to know its shape

take it out and look at it,
rub your thumb along the edge
until it snags

wet it, dry it out,
watch the changing colours
— greens,
dust off the crusted salt
from its surface,
from the ends of your fingers.

lay it on the beach

see how long you can
look at it lying in the sand

— its imprint still a red shape
in your palm —

let the tide take it.
each wave tugs it further away
before retreating.

it's still yours,
and each wave smoothes the edges some more

until you can forget about it —
carry it with you
and sometimes
put your hand in your pocket,
feel the familiar shape

take it out and look at it —
like it, even.

Unnamed - Cecilia Valensise

They wind their way through streets and streams, the
hollow of their eyes sunken in the abscess of anchored
beam. It's not the whiteness of their skins, the frays in
their jeans. It's the threat, the smack, the crack, the fear,
the mirroring of horror in a single eye's tear. Struck to
the bone marrow perished blue with cold. Fears deeper
than fearless eyes, bouncing off the high streets lands of
pounds, people in power, windows of frothed cream,
as high pitch sounds, sirens of any given London night.
They wind their ways through streets and streams. The
journey of routes, the Balkan, Libyan and the Northern
Sea silent flashes, screams of drownings future and past.

Going to Heathcote Williams's Funeral — Vanessa Vie

I/

How a Hawk flew...

— Forked are the wings

Forked is the Substance

For whom the bell tolls...

Over water

Over a single stem of Dandelion

Over lovers seeing this single stem of Dandelion

And Weeping Willows drooping
                              to touch Water

Lest death

       Death

And after-death — please... some

Signs of solace*

II/

There was a bus going to Jericho

But we/ pilgrims/ walked at water-pace

Athirst

To St. Barnabas Church

How the light shone extra brilliant

T h r o u g h   the rose window

Then I saw   inscribed on the wall

The igniting note: Cherubim & Seraphim continually do cry.

*... some Signs of solace:

Susan de Muth (Thin Man Press) has published Heathcote Williams's book "American Porn" (among others); in this book, Heathcote tells how Obama swatted a fly during a press conference.
Susan had worked hard on editing, dedicating a lot of time to this controversial book; moments after the funeral, Susan felt something in her hair to discover to her surprise, it was a dead fly.

Susan mentioned also how when Dylan Thomas died, a white cat came strolling round his resting place during the interment. Thomas used to call his wife "Cat". They are buried together.

On The Death of Heathcote Williams — Saira Viola
for Heathcote

Blue Venus of verse has left us Activist , film maker mis-
chief maker love warrior poet gentle soul musical jackal ,
magician adieu and farewell

When your magic sun comets the earth
The flame of rebellion burns
You are the song that rattles the soul
Kinky - haired poet - prophet - punk preaching
to the world
You are the final word
Red snapper rebelista !
Lyrical Spartacus - in a maze of
darkness
The sharpened needle of truth
behind the hiss of Judas
Flicker kicking with whales
Confabbing with elephants
Mischief making Puck -
inking walls and Buckingham Palace with protest -punch
graffiti
Friend to the lost- the -dispossessed   the hungry
Bob Marley tootin' Emperor of Frestonia
Aristo' don of Anarchy
Peanut brittle choco chomping British dandy!
Now that you've rocketed onto another plane
cherub -smiling   dolphins
and tear cupped - daffodils
will sink in slumber
Bonobos   and orang -utans   salute your cosmic laughter
Hot- lick word wit playa
Verses clap clap   like purple thunder
slapping ignorance -
with spanky pants intelligence
— candy pale eyes

see the air is free
You are the whispered echo of conscience
on a Dizzy Gillespie   breeze
Lexical spinning -rock god
Skin thumping the drum -spreading your
wizardry on street corners and market stalls
You are that flowering amber butterfly
back flip jibing on talking leaves
The storied power of hope on
a bike of honey bees
The blood dust of a silver- petalled star
Bless up ! Prince Fiah !
A melody of tears may twist the lips of dawn
But your electric harpsichord of love plays on.

Bastard London! (a Drunken Sermon Delivered by Rebel John Homeless Preacher. 4Am July 31st) – Saira Viola

'London is a bastard !'
In Leicester Square
Rebel John homeless preacher delivers his sermon
from a makeshift pulpit
outside an ice cream parlour
Some say the wiry long haired blackcoat
has lost his mind others embrace his chaotic diatribe .
'Who's listening to me ?' Rebel John yells
Answers his own question through splintered teeth:
'There are almost bare -assed cherry sweetie cutie pop
teens
grind winding electric- lit side streets
dressed in poly satin shimmer
bosom tops and mini skirts
Everyone stares at them
Right or wrong
Their strawberry cheeked innocence gone gone gone !
They are pointy shoe office- worker shirker 's midday
fant- a- fuck
Damson lips pillow pout ages terms and prices
In the shadows you can hear the peppered hiss of Bessim
their thorn tongued Albanian pimp
London is a sly disguise
A bitch ! Frankenstein's mistress!
Her red lick stick wetting up
swinging her ankles from Blackfriars's Bridge
wiping her clit for business
London a cloud of crippled pigeons
on a fatherless tower block
An acid attack on a kohl eyed hijabi
Yesterday's kung po chicken
A pair of period stained grass green panties lying in the
street

London you're a thread of hope to a half burned Syrian
refugee
But two whiskey punches on a black afro haired teen
Cold blooded capitalist king
Left me with two limp legs and sick-dick urine
Welcome to the starry lips of commerce
pedalling smooth tongued scams and misery
London will wed you
to debt for perpetuity
Read a suicide sonnet from the Gherkin
Saw a swiped wallet on the Northern line
And a peeping tom with red-moon eyes
I'm drunk ! Drunk! ! Drunk !
On your greasy plate of riches and cunt
London ! Fucking London ! Choking on a
toilet slurp of English Defence League HATE
A cathedral of broken promises
And wiggly finger pointing hypocrisy
Royston's colonial grandpa shows a
white gloved hand behind the palace window
You're a bleeding thumb in Whitehall
A parliament of crooks
London !The people trusted you !
 Yes you ! Bare knuckled wrestling bailiff
defecating on my porch
Stole my home ! My rights my sacred ounce of dignity
Socially cleansed jewel of inequality
Just a moped hit and run
A re -used syringe a perforated ear drum
Beware the river Thames swollen with sewage -the bitter
blood of lost souls and dead fish
London you 're a cocaine spreadsheet
stapled to Steve the banker's pumper dump
I know dirty Keith charges £50 quid a high
Brixton Baz can offer pingers peelers and e bombs to
sweeten the ride
London you're still a Dickensian hangover

Voguing cabaret singer clowning around outside
The Royal Courts of Injustice
A hot spank on that cross dressing Judge's lacy pink
g-string
An anti immigration van spot-checking a 'Muslim'
looking man
A Downtown Abbey class reunion
Fuckedupedyness in a hipster's cup
Viceland rebellion all dressed up
A bloviated dinner guest who guffaws at racist jokes
A golden ladder to paradise
but only for the darling rich-
three spoons of Beluga caviar at the Dorchester
Mouth wide open for Promenade deals with lawyers and
fixers
London how will you feed another crying bouquet of
blacktop babies ?
You are the crusted eye of depression when the day stands
still
All big talk and promises
An ad man's bubble wrapped fantasy
A drain of motionless bodies —
Sleeping on cardboard boxes
London your walls are sighing
There is a non stop train of dissension
Sprouting weedy pockets of rebellion
But is it enough to change ?
Enough to grow a conscience ?
London — a beam of silver I once believed in
Now my book of tears
A bowl of nothing .'

Yuli - David Walker

A silk summer dress
A barbed wire fence
Tiger, on a tiger skin rug
Only the aftermath proves the storm
& us, left singing in the rubble
All due ruin

Nicaragua - Mariana Saori Wall

we drove alongside the shadow
of a sleek black bird
I traced it's outline several times
until the tip of my finger
burned from the searing heat
of the dark tinted windows
outside different fences and walls
hint at what lies beyond them
barbed wire, neatly trimmed tree trunks
border barren red earth
"Radio? Por favor?"
a static political speech comes on
"Cristiana! Socialista! Solidar-"
the driver changes the station
Lil' Jon, born Jonathan Smith
Turn Down For What
Pebbles flick our van from the broken road
I close my eyes and imagine
I am in a space ship to Mars
Everyone wants shots!
navigating galactic debris
I open my eyes
we are indeed in another world
women and their daughters
proudly comb their long black hair
they work stands with religious statues
and ceramic smurfs
kermit the frog sitting on a mushroom
beyond their stand of goods
wisteria and bougainvillea
canopy gaunt white horses

Untitled - Lori Wallace

Here I am. Life's solo traveller.
Finder, keeper, and memory gatherer.
My shadow, my company, I always play safe.
Enslaving my heart, it can never act brave.

So when I met you I didn't expect.
To fall into you and truly connect.
And three seasons later, my feelings still true.
But you are gone now, and I have left too.

And so I rise to a place of faith.
With no one to hear me I send prayers into space.
Waiting for an echo that never rings through.
In the empty place that once stood you.

And the game we played was so stupid and cruel.
Yet I dream of that day, that was just me and just you.
And what I felt then, I know you felt too.
But we were afraid to say it, though we knew it was true.

And I have nothing to offer you only myself.
But I don't think I'm enough for your status and wealth.
And it may sound contrite. But to lay down with you each
day and each night.
Would be my dream, my strength, and my light.

So I drag myself on with the shadow of you.
And I make my peace, but can never forget you.
So carry on and live your life.
While I dream to be your lover, your queen or your wife.

The Language of Pain - Emily Wells

Inaudible utterings
lipless languid mouth sealed shut
while flesh gasps for breath.
Is it pain you hear? Or
ornamented reason, unrelenting
rapture, bleeding peeling
crimson fissures, the trappings
of metaphor, as you try to mimic
the world, to find that no one
is listening now.

Things I Already Knew - Emily Wells

He will hold my interest by
complimenting and insulting
me in interesting ways. The
city hanging flat as a poster
behind us is inconsequential —
we are contained under a
bell jar, porous hearts perishing.
He is touched by my flimsiness,
wants to strengthen me, but the
bones are already breaking. He will
be the first of many men to want
to teach me something. It is a
cliché to love him, but clichés
bechance vain people. Soon, I
will be spat out in fury.

The Bedroom Philosophers - Emily Wells

Perhaps you think you've awakened a demon in me,
that if someone were to search for where the damage
was done they would find you as the instrument

Or you think you are always with me, twine around my
ankle
fidgeting remains after our mouths were emptied of sweet
blood
But you are not apocalyptic anymore.

When I dream of you it is a glass dream
Your physical exactness blurred in steam — now, stasis
My resurrectionist's eyes are nothing like deliverance.

I laugh and demand a new tyrant. Beware the common
horror show, the woman who smiles without dedication. I
cannot help but be near wildness now. It is a kind of
cleanliness

I left you in a drawer of memory, never full.
My body mixes you bodily with blood, and
will scatter you like feathering petals on the walk to its
tomb.

Clarity: your legacy. I tried to write a book about my
body,
but I was really writing about how many times men
have almost killed me.

Breathing - Cicely Whitehead

Whatever this is
This right now
All consuming and turbulent
Ship-wrecking your soul in sudden
waves of tummy-flipping fury
and a head clouding mercurial
being

It
Will
Pass
Over as if dust brushed off the
Surface
revealing again the sun and your
smile
Because you are here.
Open your eyes to the constancy of
hillsides, of toes in sand, of sunsets
fading to midnight blue allover this earth.
Breathe me in
I am your constancy
Your river, ravine, waterfall.
Comets should strike before my
rocky formation crumbles,
Meteors will shower the surface
before the flow falters
and my pulse alters
direction.
Breathe me in —
the blossom
and the grasses
and the fire
and the brook
that passes
through your veins
in an immovable feast.
In
and out.

The End of Summer - Alice Whiting

Lying around making love to the day
with the memory
of
so many lovers
on my mind
my legs open wide
I remember voices
lips
finger tips
and in gazing at the blue sky
I can see my sighs
in the shapes of the clouds.

Fossils - Alice Whiting

We would walk in the shingle
The wind blowing our hair like a malevolent spirit
salt in our eyes and lips dry
You showed me how to push the stones with one hand like
a wave
first up
then down
to reveal the sharks teeth
fossils.
Once I found a meteorite
I held it in my wet glove mottled with sand and grit,
a treasure.
Seaweed sat in dark knotted clumps.
When the sun broke through the clouds
and shone gold beams onto the water
I remembered religious paintings
I had seen on our holidays in France.
The ancient dry hollow taste of the churches
Had the same sweetness
as the wooden box on top of the fireplace
where you kept our relics from the beach.
I remember the cuts on your feet
when you waded out to retrieve me from a rock as the tide
was coming in,
And the ever changing colours of the sky
with the rolling clouds
and endless horizon
blue like our veins
blue like the fishing nets
as blue as our lips
when we ran dripping from the sea.

Sicilian Descent London Boy - Alice Whiting

Sewing down the front of my blouse
so my tits don't pop out
Eating nothing for dinner
And rushing out the door
Half an hour late
In high heels
To meet Jack
He's the Sicilian descent London boy
With sad black eyes and eye lashes like a horse
He's wearing a brown leather jacket
And calls it an organised fashion crime
He kisses my thighs because he loves my legs
and pushes his face into my breasts while I sit on his lap
His mouth at my armpits
He breathes in my sweat
Because he's the kind of guy that wants to bury his face
between a woman's legs till he suffocates
Animal hard he's hot in his jeans and they fill out in the
most pornographic way
And I go home feeling depressed in my tight white blouse
High heels hurt
I have to get up early
And there was nowhere for us to fuck.
Above all of this
And most pressingly
I'm pretty certain
He doesn't love me.

Lately — Alice Whiting

The ceilings are higher here.
The windows wider
the bathrooms whiter
the jewellery golder.
My heart beats faster
my voice laughs louder
but my mind feels flat lined.
Things I would have felt guilty for before
no longer torment me
because I don't care anymore.
And some people say I have changed.
I've seen the way the damned live back home
I've seen the way the beautiful live in my new home
it's not so different.
Pill boxes are still made of plastic
It is only my exterior that has become jewel encrusted.
These days I forget to return calls
and to ask the time of day
The weeks are a haze of champagne and three course meals
from a take away.
Sometimes I clean up his kitchen for him
when he holds me I am lost in a pungent glow
of testosterone, washing powder and the new fragrance
from Valentino.
Friends from back home tell me I am looking great
and my existence is rated by the amount of likes on my
facebook page
from people I don't even know
or recognise.
I found a toy boy in a platinum play pen
where only limited edition and narcotics can satisfy him.
There is a mountain of disinteresting interest
which we ignore
And the red letter from my subconscious is thrown into
the rubbish
with scraps of my personality
and the contents
of last nights ash tray.

Vows - Simon Widdop

One sparked up a fresh Richmond under the glow of the
heat lamp, the other puffed away on a menthol grape vape
that scented the shelter
The stubborn silence was broken with an offhand com-
ment on the rain. He smirked, snorted and agreed but
still seemed out of the moment
Another heavy drag on the dark blue electric fag in his
hand
Through thick and thin, for better or for worse, in sick-
ness
and in health
they'd sworn it
When he walked in again to find her on the bed again
with the bottles emptied again and coursing of crimson
across her wrists again which meant the nurses again which
meant wait
 after wait after wait for a referral again the world become
colder again and the cycle was starting over again
He knew he needed to stick it out, he could never make
this worse
the lust was gone, but he couldn't walk away
maybe this time she'll beat it
maybe this time
maybe

When The Revolution Comes - Simon Widdop

When the revolution comes
will it be bloody and glorious?
the Marxists and the anarchists
shaking off the shackles of oppression to a symphony of
tourettes syndrome gunfire
spewing forth from the mouths of the barricades
When the revolution comes
will it pass peacefully?
the spiritual ones and the pacifists
forming human chain row on row on row stretching mo-
torways and Lay Lines
from Land's End to the Isle Of White
When the revolution comes
will it be done through great talk and great debate?
the people united away from keyboard warriors away from
safe spaces away from buzzword insults
united together to heal the wounds of divide and to fight
those that divide us
When the revolution comes
I'll be ready for the change
so choose your path Brother, choose your path Sister
and I'll see you there

I – Elizabeth Jane Whitton

I am defined by gaps & creases
that have been carved into me
like the bark of a wise old tree

I remember the days
That made me bitter
Too bright, like an empty room
Harsh, overwhelming dew

I am pushing the vacuum
out in all directions, tired tendrils
I am caressing the void
like an old lover

I wear these thoughts like a flimsy jacket
Maybe it's an heirloom, a thrifted find or an ancient arti-
fact
Either way, I know it doesn't fit quite right.

Paradise - Elizabeth Jane Whitton

We're the periphery
The little buildings
Nobody sees when they
Beach themselves on piles of trash

We're the ones that feed the monster when it needs bar-
tenders, dancers, smiling faces
It chews small bills
And mosquito bites
We're the ones who will wait on you when you're overripe

The Last Dodo — Heathcote Williams

"Why," said the Dodo, *"the best way to explain it is to do it."*
— Lewis Carroll, Alice's Adventures in Wonderland

Lewis Carroll was nicknamed the Dodo
Because of his inveterate stutter.
Asked his name, he'd reply 'Do-Do-Dodgson'.
He found 'Carroll' easier to utter.

So Charles Lutwidge Dodgson, the clergyman,
Became Lewis Carroll, author of distinction,
Who'd revive the Dodo in his 'Alice in Wonderland' —
The real Dodo having suffered from extinction.

For Lewis Carroll had been very intrigued
By something he'd seen in a Museum:
A large-cropped bulbous bird that was stuffed
And could be seen in the old Ashmolean.

Two hundred years before a Dodo had been captured
By sailors stopping off in Mauritius.
They'd thought it part goose, part vulture and were fearful
—
Sailors being naturally superstitious.

But the bird was fearless and easily lured aboard
By an offer of unlimited ship's biscuits.
By a miracle the bird survived the crew's curiosity
And their wondering if it tasted delicious.

After it had lived out its life in England
A taxidermist was called when it died.
He stuffed it and, to retain its luxuriant plumage,
Cunning preservatives were applied.

The first owner in its afterlife was John Tradescant,
Who passed it onto Elias Ashmole,

Since when this comical but salutary creature
Has become a curator of the earth's soul.

For through it man's begun to learn that extinction
Can last for the rest of time;
And he can wistfully cherish a creature whose life
Was ended by a carnivorous crime.

A Dutch sailor, Volkert Evertsz, described the bird
As showing concern for its fellow creature:
"When I held one, he cried and others ran forward
To help the bird that was held prisoner."

In 'Wonderland' the Dodo's portrayed as benign
Given its invention of a 'caucus race'
In which everyone entering ends up winning
And accordingly is then given a prize.

People say that something's "as dead as a Dodo"
As if relishing the gentle giant's demise,
Yet it lives on as an innocent victim of that progress
Which prefers sunset to a hopeful sunrise.

The Dodo may have died out from being too nice;
Large and flightless with an excess of trust.
Those who last saw it alive in the seventeenth century
Said the Dodo was friendly. And now it's dust.

When it was alive it was briefly displayed in London
As part of an urban freak show.
In death it has become a testament to the folly of man,
More deserving of derision than the Dodo.

For years the Ashmolean was an uncategorised jumble:
The Museum was nicknamed the 'knicknackatory'.
It was crammed with curios such as Guy Fawkes' lantern
But the Dodo was the star with its poignant story.

There Has To Be An Afterlife — Heathcote Williams

There has to be an afterlife, since matter
Can neither be created nor destroyed.
So, fear not, you'll continue. According to physics
Your future presence is definitely required.

Look, here's an atom once breathed by Socrates;
There's another breathed by Van Gogh.
Inhale deeply, you can morph into a Neanderthal.
Every second new afterlives are kicking off.

The physicist, Ilya Prigognine, believed that atoms
Make conscious decisions in a conscious existence,
Enabling the atomic thoughts in your head that are you
To enjoy an immortal persistence.

His theory means that the 'now' can go on forever,
And that its swirling thought forms may linger —
So essential distillations of our substance can be saved
From their falling victim to fate's fickle finger.

Does all this conceal a road-bump for atheists?
Could it hide an inconvenient truth?
Do invisible parts of our being possess
Encrypted secrets of eternal youth?

When Vincent van Gogh was studying the Milky Way
With candles perched on his hat
He meditated on each billion-year-old shining dot
Spinning through the starry night.

He believed that the heavens were our future destination
And he declared, "we take death to reach a star."
Now that there's stardust in every single cell of our body
More mystery is added to knowing who we are.

But in bereavement it's a very great comfort
To those who are feeling dispossessed
To consider that those they've known who've died
Have simply changed their cosmic address.

Castro's Room — Jan Woolf

'Good evening El Commandant.'

'Good evening, comrade.'

'Your room is ready.'

'Thank you, I'm tired.'

'Of course,' says the Third Secretary, turning the brass handle of the elegant oak door, welcoming the big man across the threshold. There's no need to snap on a light, for a candle gutters on the small table in the corner, throwing out comforting shadows.

'I'd like to be alone now comrade.'

'Certainly El Commandant,' says the Third Secretary, dipping his head in respect, 'have a comfortable night.'

The door closes, its reverse side as rough and splintered as the outside is smooth and polished. On the uneven dirt floor, a narrow mattress on straw. Two blankets with gaudy patterns of lemons cover a hemp sheet. No pillow. On another table, a jug of water stands in a chipped enamel bowl, a cloth over it. The wall is the same earth colour as the floor, and a crack zigzags down it, like a streak of brown lightning. On one side of the crack hangs a small crucifix in vivid colours, and the on other, a framed black and white photograph of Lenin in full throat, addressing the St Petersburg crowds, his finger pointing directly at the suffering Christ. The hemp curtains are drawn, concealing no light, but an inner brick wall. In another corner, on top of a square of cracked linoleum, squats a bucket with a lid, a roll of toilet paper beside it, perhaps the room's only luxury. El Commandant walks across the room, sighing with pleasure. At peace now, and tired from the embassy dinner and chit-chat, this time with Norwegians; politics, culture, world peace, cigars. He lies on the mattress, stretching his legs, knowing he'd sleep well tonight. For this was his room, and every embassy in the world has one just like it.

Navaswan — Jan Woolf

When the cold air of night meets the warmth of the coming day, a breeze ripples around the earth. This is the leading edge of dawn. Very few are aware of its existence or multiple layers of colour. In India it's called the Navaswan. It makes the birds sing, and all the yogis wake up. One of them, who long ago became a Sadhu, welcomed his 43,440th Navaswan in the mouth of his cave. A lot had happened during his 110 years. All of the sounds of nature that form his language had been mastered, his senses refined, but his organs have withered like prunes. He can barely stand, the berries and nuts that keep him alive have become less digestible, yet he knows every insect, bird, scrap of dust: every sound of the weather, sunshine, snowfall and wind. He's become them, and there are no flaws in him now as he approaches perfection — a heartbeat away from the absolute he longs for. But he has not enough strength for his own action. What can a man do who can only be?

He hears a new sound, a rustling at the mouth of his cave. A man wearing strange clothes: tight blue trousers, cotton shirt and shoes that look like flashing fish. One of the city men.
'I own this land,' says the man, as he enters.
'This is my cave,' said the Sadhu.
'This place is to be dynamited, and I want you out.'
'Oh?'
'I'll put you in a home where you'll be happy.'
'I'm already happy.'
'I'll do everything I can to keep you comfortable.'
'I have an idea that will help us both,' says the squatting Sadhu, his eyes twinkling. 'Yes?' Says the city man.
'My voice is weak, let me whisper to you, bend down.'
As the man bends, the Sadhu picks up a stick, raises it with

all the strength he has left, and hits the man on the head.
'I'll never leave. Now go away, you dog.'
The man leaves, holding his head and his shame.

Just after the next Navaswan, the man appears at the
mouth of the cave, a shotgun under his arm. As he
points the gun, the Sadhu's heart explodes with happi-
ness, his arms outstretched in a wingspan of joy.

Eulogy for a Defiant Gardener — Jan Woolf

1955

'Pruned the raspberries Cremton?'

'Fuck 'orf M'lady.' Your delayed response after straightening yourself as best you could, leaning on your spade, tugging at your cap, me in the wheelbarrow, Lady Roseberry out of earshot. I was five, but old enough to know that fuck 'orf was rude. But so was she. Your name was Crampton, not Cremton. Fred Crampton, my dad. You were always nice to her face though, for we needed the tied cottage, your job in his Lordship's kitchen garden, and Mum's as a cleaner. Lord and Lady Raspberry you called them. Of course you'd pruned the raspberries - which you called Roseberries — with care and skill, knowing just where to nick them with the secateurs so they'd make fruit in the summer. I loved that kitchen garden. And I loved you.

You were only thirty-six, but Mum said you'd come back oldened by the war, from a place called Dun-Kirk. 'Dunked 'im in the sea right enough, but at least he made it 'ome, not like some poor buggars,' Mum told me one teatime, after I'd asked about the war and what you'd done. She told me that my birth had put the spring back in the crooked step that drove your wheelbarrow along the gravel paths, between the box hedges of the kitchen garden with the rows of beetroot, their maroon leaves shimmying in the breeze, and the carrots growing in powder fine earth. Earth that I helped you pick the stones from. 'Why do we have to take the stones out of the dirt Daddy?'

'The roots grow crooked if they hit a stone, Floss.'

'Did your leg ever hit a stone Dad? Is that why you limp?'

'Something like that Flossy. But you can't keep a good bloke down,' you'd joked, rolling a cigarette. I'd clung to your neck, laughing. You smelled of tobacco and grass.

We planted potatoes too, spuds you called them, some earlies, some lates, but they all looked the same to me, chitting in their boxes, growing fat scabby shoots. You let me use the dibber, poking the broad stick into the ground. But my child's hands could never push it in far enough. Every time I made a hole, lumps of earth fell in, just where the spud should go. Later - much later - after you'd told me what had happened, I knew that earthing them up in the funereal mounds that made their leaves struggle for the light, reminded you of the earthing up of your dead comrades. 'I was the last man standing,' you told me, when I was old enough to hear.

1959

When I was nine, you let me pull the cabbages and pick the dark green stuff that tasted of flannels. Kale. Then there were the knobbly Brussels sprouts that Mum would boil for half an hour. 'Puts 'airs on yer chest,' you said.

'What Dad, airs like you said M'lady had?'

'No Floss, that's hairs and graces.' And you'd laughed, even though your leg hurt. I loved the runner beans, growing up their poles. Looking for them among the leaves, green on green, appearing like magic skinny grass snakes. They were M'lady's beans, but you'd planted your lady's beans - broad beans - in a line between the rows. 'Broad like yer mum's backside,' you'd chuckled, 'but don't tell 'er I said.'

'I won't Dad.'

'We need a Labour government,' you'd declared. 'Till then I'll plant our beans down the middle, an' I don't care what they think.'

'What's a Labour Government?'

'Nothing to do with Lord and Lady Raspberry, that's for sure.'

Then there were the onions, throttled in dirt, their long green whiskers reaching for the sky, surrendering like

defeated soldiers. You'd sang a song 'I'm a lonely little
petunia in an onion patch.' I liked that song, but you'd
looked sad; lonely like the petunia, I thought — the last
man standing. We'd pull the onions in the autumn,
make a knot in their whiskers and put them on a sieve to
dry in the shed; a paradise of murk and surprise. There
were nests of mice in there, woodlice, and cobwebs as
thick as your socks.

I loved the greenhouse too, the trailing hosepipes, its
misty hissing air, that peaty smell, the sharp tang of to-
mato. It felt like another country. Your glasses would
steam up, but your leg felt better in the warm, you said.
Later, after you'd told me what had happened, I imagined
you staunching the wounds of a comrade with the same
care that you'd tied the tomato plants against their canes.
I remember you rescuing a frog that had plopped into the
water tank and couldn't get out, falling back, and back,
into the water, its useless arms with no purchase against
the dank, black metal. Were you, in your mind, fishing
that desperate man out of the sea? His mouth agape, eyes
bloodshot. The man you finally told me about? The one
that you'd decided could live?

We'd hear soft thuds as apples made their way through
lattice works of leaves, and onto the ground. A gentle,
reassuring sound, but sometimes you'd jump. I asked
you why, but you'd lit another cigarette and, brightening,
changed the subject. 'It's called scrumping, Floss, when
you take an apple that no-one wants, to keep it from the
maggots.' And we'd put ripe ones in our pockets. 'But
don't tell M'lady.'
    'I promise Dad.'
After most of the apples had fallen, the clocks went back.
'Winter drawers on eh Floss?' And I'd laugh, loving the
smell of bonfires, the smoke curling into the evening air.
We'd look up together, at the remaining apples hanging

on like moons in the bare branches. Such happiness.

1963

When I was thirteen, and you forty-four - getting on
Flossy - I crunched a snail under my foot. I laughed,
when once I'd have cried at such wanton murder. But it
was dead already, like the rest of the snails that had ma-
noeuvred round the flowerpots. You'd looked sombre.
'They look like burned out tanks.'
'You mean water tanks, Dad?'
          'No, the ones I saw at Dunkirk.'
'Will you tell me about that?'
          'One day Floss, one day.' And then we lobbed
snails like hand grenades over the wall onto M'lady's
flowerbeds, laughing hysterically. Sometimes we 'd fill
a bucket with them. And chuck them into the compost,
where they fell like shrapnel. I found out about shrapnel
of course, how poor old Len had caught some in the neck,
dying in front of you on the beach. 'He never even said
goodbye Floss, nor passed on a message for his ma.' But
you'd gone to see her anyway, telling her that he never had
any pain, and passing on his love before his eyes closed.
Old Len was twenty-one.

We'd put horseshit on the rhubarb, its brown orbs re-
minding you of M'lady's hairdo.
It made their leaves flourish and spread. I picked them for
umbrellas to keep off the rain. 'You'd better wash your
hands Floss, rhubarb leaves are bad for you.'
          'How come?'
          'They just are.'
          'How come?'
          'They're poison.'
          'Why?'
          'Dunno, but I want nothing, nothing in this world
that is bad for you. It's yours now, Flossy.'
          'The rhubarb?'

'The world.'
'Oh. Does your leg hurt today?'
'A bit.'

The prickly Gooseberry bushes with their hairy fruit
grew against the wall. You once told me, winking, that
I was found underneath one. 'Dad, I was never.' For I
was thirteen and beyond the birds and the bees by way
of explanation, but I didn't let on that I knew how I was
made. The gooseberries were delicious when snot yellow,
and soft enough to spurt their pips if squeezed. I giggled,
thinking about my friends in the school playground.

We discovered strawberries together, their chins rest-
ing on the straw, like jewels. We could have as many as
we liked because no-one, apart from us, knew they were
there, behind the mint.
'Why do you plant mint in buckets Dad?'
'To stop it spreading.'
'Why?'
You'd looked stricken. 'Terrible if it spreads.'
'What?'
'I don't want any of that for you, Floss,' you'd said,
shaking your head.
'What do you mean?' I'd felt stones in my tummy.
For I knew that something was happening far away, in
Cuba, to do with the Russians and Americans. And for
the first time in the kitchen garden I saw your fear. I
didn't know what to do. Find you some raffia? A bucket?
A dibber? I unscrewed your flask, pouring out the hot,
sweet tea and you reassured me. 'Don't you worry Floss,
nothing's going to spread.' And I felt safe again.

1968

One summer evening, rinsed in birdsong, I came to see
you in the kitchen garden, loving you as much as ever I

did. You were forty-nine, I, a woman of eighteen wearing my stripy tee shirt and white jeans. 'Look at you Flossy, the bees knees, mind you don't stain them trousers,' you'd said, as I brushed by the raspberry canes, the fruit falling at a touch.
'What's in that letter love?' you'd asked.
'From the university Dad, I got in.'
'That's my clever girl, let's have some roseberries to celebrate.'
 I picked and ate, picked and ate, and then dropped one, the blotch of a stain — blood red against white — blooming on my thigh.   You flinched, and wept — and then finally told - of the soldier who was your best friend, who'd died beside you at Dunkirk. And later on that terrible day, leaning over the edge of that brave little fishing boat, pulling the other man out of the sea, the one that you'd decided could live.

You dried your tears. 'Sorry Floss, but better out than in.'
     'Yes Dad.'
     'University eh? Proud of you.'
We'd hooked arms, and looked together at the ancient apple trees, rooted like guardian angels by the stone arch of the kitchen garden. A wind set them dancing, and you'd raised your face to them, in homage to life, and in your eyes I thought I saw joy, and a defiance of what you knew.

In the Shadow of the Light — Hugo Zeehyena

Wise words empty spaces
Lonely lanterns on the black lake
So many days to fill with nights
So much daze and so little calm
Oppositions on narrow webs

Look out and look inside
Behind those trees remains a lie
Besides your voice I hear no cry
A common lament for the longing
A blue car gone by midnight.

In the dewy grass you stretch
'Morning love' and goodnight hay
Time is misconveived but
Not as much as your heart is

Shaking through the dust
Alone in the bush
Dancing pillows in the house
Shivering art and breaking heart.

Upon our misery there is a kind of mystery
Chemistry lost within felony
Set up a trial on the double bed

Kidding or living the best is existing
Love's uttered like a billion other words
That some languages don't speak.

The world is too big for you
Even though you're coming through

Volcanoes were made to kill

Our spider-shaped lonelinesses.

You heard something squeezing
It was probably my heart
You heard something dying
The burning sun in your back.

Going Backwards in the Moving Silence - Hugo Zeehyena

We're like wolves in the dreaded night
Hungover but still ready to fight
Going backwards in the moving silence
Finding strength in the turbulence
Loneliness is a dark knight
Sublime and sad in the moonlight.

I buried my heavy heart
In the sandy shores of yours
And the frozen tide
Keeps me from getting it back.

Well you turned into something
And it made me feel like I was nothing
Going backwards in the moving silence
Trying to stay afloat despite the violence
Of them rampaging and forwarding
Letters announcing the death of a king.

And that's why
Young hearts lock themselves
In the night
There comes silence
Sirens keep on singing
Melodies of sorrow
Keep me away from the past
And the death of the oceans.

All them sad eyes
Keeping faith for years
Trainwrecks have been pushed aside
For the rocket to be launched
Time and space will collide
In the hands of the dark

All videos will be silent
And join their tired ancestors
All books will be scattered
In the unforgiving wind
The crowds will move on
In their eternal lie
And the doomed will keep on
Going backwards in the moving silence
From the hills they will heal
And hold their dreams as their will.

LISTENING TO JAMES,
'GETTING AWAY WITH IT
(ALL MESSED UP)'

nothing matters
life's complete

completely meaningless

for f*ck's sake I'm 53

farting out these word salads
contentedly

SPACE FOR YOUR OWN POEMS HERE :

SPACE FOR YOUR OWN POEMS HERE :

SPACE FOR YOUR OWN POEMS HERE :

SPACE FOR YOUR OWN POEMS HERE :

SPACE FOR YOUR OWN POEMS HERE :

NEW RIVER
PRESS

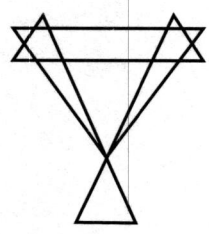

FITZROVIA
LONDON